the
disciple
diaries

To order additional copies of *The Disciple Diaries*, by Ray Minner, **call 1-800-765-6955.**

Visit us at www.reviewandherald.com for information on other Review and Herald® products.

the
disciple
diaries

teen devotional

ray minner

ⁱR

REVIEW AND HERALD® PUBLISHING ASSOCIATION
HAGERSTOWN, MD 21740

This book was
Edited by Gerald Wheeler
Copyedited by James Cavil and Delma Miller
Designed by Trent Truman
Cover photo by Getty Images
Electronic makeup by Shirley M. Bolivar
Typeset: 12/15 Bembo

PRINTED IN U.S.A.

09 08 07 06 05   5 4 3 2 1

R&H Cataloging Service
Minner, Ray Deane, 1949-
    The disciple diaries.

    1. Christian life.   2. Teenagers—Prayer books
and devotionals.

                    243.63

ISBN 0-8280-1839-1

Dedication

To Jennifer, Megan, Katie, and Caleb,
who make being a dad my greatest honor . . .

. . . and to Karen,
who waits for Jesus now, but whose memory
still sweetens every day.

The Karen Minner Scholarship Fund

Every spring the Minner family awards a scholarship of $1,000 to a student, chosen by the faculty of Highland View Academy in Hagerstown, Maryland, who exhibits the qualities of Christian character seen in Karen's life, who maintains a high grade point average, and who models leadership and active participation in campus life at HVA, as Karen did.

To learn more about Karen and this scholarship, visit **www.KarenMinner.com.**

Contents

Introduction

Note to the Reader:

The italic portions of this book are John speaking directly to the reader. The regular print is my voice. Each chapter will begin with John's perspective, based on his experience with Jesus. Then I will address various current teen issues, such as parent relationships, peer relationships, understanding God's will for teens in our popular culture, etc. (I had also considered touching on some of the specific temptations we always suppose teens are dealing with, such as sexual activity, drug use, etc., but the research I have conducted among three different groups of kids indicates that typical readers of this book are not likely to be struggling with those things. They are far more interested in learning how to get along with their parents and care properly for their friends in a spiritual context.)

Then the book will conclude with John as an old man reflecting on his lifetime of serving Jesus.

chapter 1

The Call
by the Sea

Decisions are not usually hard for me. Even in my youth I could make choices easily without worrying whether I had done the right thing. Of course, it wasn't that way with some of my friends. Fortunately, in our village we didn't find ourselves confronted with a barrage of choices to make daily. Our lives were pretty predictable.

Only three places were central to my life: the lake, the shore where we moored our fishing boat, and home. I had long ago finished my schooling. Except for the Sabbath my days all began and ended with a sameness that promised to continue throughout the rest of my life. Contemplating my future, I knew I could look forward to a lot of fish.

Our business focused mostly on the northern end of the lake, prime territory for the tilapia and other fish we shipped daily to Jerusalem and Caesarea. As long as fish remained a staple of the diet for Jews, Samaritans, Romans, and the other ethnic groups we traded with (and the authorities continued to renew our contract to fish for them, since they owned the rights to the fish in the lake), we would be in fine shape. Naturally, we depended on a bountiful supply of fish, but nature almost always provided for us.

My father, Zebedee, my brother James, and I took a lot of pride in our profession, including the way we treated our employees. Zebedee Fishing Enterprises was well known throughout Judea as a good outfit to work for. We weren't wealthy by any means (and never could be, because the fish in the lake were government property), but we managed a decent living, and we enjoyed the respect of our customers and competitors alike.

Oh, I'm sorry. I haven't introduced myself properly. I'm telling you all about my life, and you don't even know me yet. I'm John.

Nothing would have set me apart from any of the other boys who lived by that lake. We would run down to the lakeshore the moment we sensed any excitement under way, whether it was a boat collision or rumors of a really big school of fish in the area. Sometimes it was fun just to watch those big storms roll in across the lake, with the amazing lightning streaks and cool whitecaps rushing to shore and even the gusts of wind that would almost knock you down.

I say it was fun, but it was a little scary, too, because every now and then some family from Bethsaida or Capernaum or Tiberias would learn that their boat didn't make it through the storm. We always ran first to our mooring spot to make sure Father was still safe.

James and I would help him every afternoon as he and his crew prepared for a night on the lake. (Well, actually, first we would check to see what food Mother was sending out with them and help ourselves to the sample Father pretended not to know we always took. Then we would assist him.)

And that's pretty much how our days passed. Then suddenly we were old enough to work full-time on the fishing boats.

Growing up in Galilee simply meant that one day you might be a student of Rabbi Horshon's and the next you were spending the first day of the rest of your life in your father's stable or vineyard or shop—in our case, on our father's boat.

I had become accustomed to the routine. It was physically demanding and the hours were long, but we would never have expected anything else. After all, it was our life. We followed the plan.

Everyone followed the plan.

As the years have passed, people have asked many times how someone like me, who knew only about following, became a leader. I always tell them how gentle and gradual and simple it was. It began the day I came ashore and looked into the eyes of a Man who calmly said, "Follow Me."

That moment divides everything that has ever happened in my life. I still see Him standing there onshore, still remember the way His hair moved in the wind.

At first I wasn't sure whether He was speaking to James or me. Really, we were both rather busy at the moment. Neither of us had time to chat. But if you've ever seen Jesus—I mean, really looked at Him—you know how difficult He is to ignore. So before we even realized what was happening, my brother and I were face to face with the Man who would change . . . everything.

We talked for only a few moments. And as the years have passed I have long forgotten exactly what He said. I just knew at once that I wanted to be with Him. He talked about making us "fishers of men," and He spoke of us as "disciples." And even though we weren't sure what that meant, we knew instinctively that what He had on His mind that morning would carry us far beyond Galilee into a life that we had never dreamed of.

Looking back, it's hard to believe we weren't more skeptical, or at least cautious. But any doubts we might have had just could not withstand the conviction in His face. I wouldn't call it stern determination, if that is what you're picturing. It was more a serene assurance that He was on a critically important mission. If He wanted us to be a part of that mission, we, incredibly, were ready. Just like that. Decision made.

I could tell you what that meant for me, but right now it might be a good idea for you to give some thought to what it will mean for you. No, not my decision—your decision. Because if Jesus has never confronted you and offered to make you His disciple, He will. Count on it.

When James and I decided to follow Jesus that day, we left everything behind—our boats, our nets, even the previous night's catch. We sacrificed it all to start down a new path. Is that what Jesus wants you to do?

Exactly what is involved in becoming a young twenty-first-century disciple of Jesus? Why would anyone want to do that? What are the risks? What do you think your life will be like after you spend some time walking beside Him through the gym and cafeteria, the mall, the shop where you work after school? Are you ready to be surprised? Are you prepared to discover qualities you never knew you had?

On the day that Jesus comes calling, you stand at a fork. Beneath Galilee's bright sky that morning I turned my back on the ordinary.

What does a disciple look like? How do you even know if you're talking to one? You probably have a picture that springs immediately to mind when you first hear the word. So I asked a few teens to describe a disciple.

"He has dark-brown eyes and a big nose," Jordyn said. "He's kind of short and round, and he wears a stupid green-and-brown robe with a sash on his head." She completed the picture with brown leather sandals and a walking stick, and in her mind he was about 45 years old.

Mindi pictured someone taller and skinnier with messy brown hair and who needed a bath!

Shawn had given it a little more thought, and his disciple had "truthful eyes" and a compassionate face framed by longish hair. The face wore a serene expression, but the eyes were "excited." His disciple, like Jordyn's, wore what they considered Middle Eastern dress.

Their ideas may be typical of those of most people. We grew up reading books illustrated with pictures of Jesus surrounded by characters just like that. At Eastertime the TV networks pull out all the old movies about Jesus' life, and sure enough, there are the disciples—Jordyn's and Mindi's and Shawn's and nine others just like them.

But did you realize that John was likely in his teens when Jesus called him? If he were a disciple of the twenty-first century, he could be a member of your high school class.

As an academy teacher I see dozens of kids in the hall every day—in the library, the parking lot, the computer lab—who could have been John. Or James. Or Andrew. Or Martha.

I see some who could have been Mary Magdalene too. Some who could have been Judas.

Why did John and James and Andrew and Martha make the choices they made? What shaped Mary Magdalene's decisions?

Ashley and Justin and Brooke and Matt each bring their baggage from home and family, from school failure or success, from stress and problems with peer acceptance, and they each stand at the same fork where choices take place. Twenty centuries after John, Jesus still waits at the spot where He finds us and says, "Follow Me."

Why do some teens drop everything and come, while others hesitate, looking longingly back at the lake and the fish, and still others respond with anger that He would ever expect anything from them?

We know what John's choice was. Let's look at the consequences.

chapter 2

Wedding at Cana

The first couple days with Jesus are just a blur now. I remember scenes of leisurely walks through the small villages of Galilee, and long silences, punctuated by bursts of eager discussion at those times when He would mention a Scripture text and then talk to us for perhaps a half hour about what it meant. He always seemed to be searching, and every so often He would stop to engage a stranger or two in conversation. Sometimes the chats ended with an invitation to "follow Me," the same call He had offered to my brother and me—and always the response was immediate. Men who had never seen Him before joined us, until we were quite a little entourage following Him down the road. Those closest to Him were in a better position to hear everything He said. But everyone jockeyed for those spots, so those who ended up in the back of the group often contented themselves with getting acquainted with each other and speculating about our destination.

Camping beside the road was a new adventure for some of us. James and I were accustomed to working all night on the lake, but we always knew we had a bed at home waiting for us when we finished our work. In the life we were now beginning this would not always be so.

On the third day we learned that we would be attending a wedding feast that evening. Weddings can be a lot of fun, of course, but only if they involve your friends, family, or neighbors. James and I had never gone to a wedding of strangers, and the thought made us a little uncomfortable. Social small talk doesn't come naturally to most fishermen. I wondered why they would even want all of us there.

We arrived to discover the festivities already well under way. The host did his best to make us feel welcome. He offered us places at the banquet tables along with all the other guests. In fact, extending their hospitality seemed especially important to the family, who, it seemed, were friends of Jesus' mother, Mary.

We had not met Mary before. But Jesus had spoken of her. And when He stepped across the threshold into the courtyard of that home, she sprang to life. We could see at once the intensity of their connection. After their first greeting her eyes continued to follow Him around the room as He visited with their friends.

As we had feared, we soon became bored. We wished the happy couple well, of course, but really, why were we here? We could have stayed in camp while Jesus put in an appearance to congratulate His friends.

Suddenly, loud and angry voices came from the servants' work area. Guests had started to line up at the punch bowl for refills, and the line wasn't moving very fast. The festive atmosphere began to grow a bit edgy.

Mary was the first to turn to Jesus. Since that night I've asked myself many times how she could have known that He would be the solution. Rushing over to Him where He was sitting in quiet conversation with Andrew, she said, "Son, there is no more wine! This is terrible! The Zormaths are going to be humiliated. Please, do something!"

Historians will tell you that pivotal events with lasting significance often come with no warning. I was there, and I can tell you that nothing signaled to us that we were about to witness something that would go down through the centuries as evidence of God's power.

In spite of His mother's obvious agitation, Jesus remained calm and did not refuse her request. I would learn later that serenity amid confusion was part of His character—indeed, something He would offer to all of us.

To Mary, knowing Jesus meant assurance that nothing further was necessary. This was her Son. And with no further discussion she rounded up the servants and told them to follow His instructions.

I listened as He spoke to them. Jesus did not hem and haw around, made no hesitant "Well, let's see now . . ." Authority filled His voice. He knew exactly what He was going to do. It suddenly occurred to me that He had been sitting at that table, conversing with Andrew, just waiting for this moment. This was why we had come!

He ordered six huge stone pots filled with water. James and Andrew and Peter and I sat together watching this little drama while the Zormaths hovered about anxiously, coaching the servants in every little move. The pots were big. It took several minutes to complete the task. By the time they had finished they had brought more than 150 gallons of water in from the well and poured it into those giant pots.

Realizing that this crowd would not happily accept water as a beverage, I was becoming a bit apprehensive as the exhausted servants mopped up the spilled water around the pots. Was this what Jesus had to offer? This was how He was going to take care of it?

"Dip some out and take it to the steward," Jesus said. At that moment I wanted to be far away from the wedding.

"Amazing!" boomed the steward's voice across the courtyard. Not realizing where this "wine" had come from, he turned to the bride-

groom and began raving about how unusual it was to save the best wine for later in the feast.

"You have outdone yourself, sir!" he fairly shouted.

The line at the punch bowl began to move once again, and the dancing resumed. Jesus returned to His conversation with Andrew.

Somehow Mary had known. She had never seen Him do anything comparable before, but she had confidence in Him. As for us, once we grasped what we had seen, we understood that we had seen God at work, suspending even natural laws through this man. I wish I could say that we learned to trust Him that night.

Trusting Jesus completely—understanding that circumstances never overwhelmed Him—would take a while longer.

In the broad scope of Jesus' ministry on earth, the miracle at the wedding feast stands apart from almost everything else. It has no obvious connection to God's plan of sacrificing His Son to save us from sin. There seem to be no life-and-death issues. It was just a party that went bad, probably because of poor planning. We've all been to parties that have turned a little lame. Usually the guests just sneak glances at their watches and wonder if it's too late to go somewhere else. People get over it.

I suspect that Jesus chose a wedding party for His first miracle precisely because it was such a common event. The private home of a Galilean family, where hospitality was so critically important, was the perfect venue for God to demonstrate His regard for us. The Zormaths (or whatever their name was) were undoubtedly not wealthy people. The occasion of their child's marriage would have been a high point in their lives. And even in today's Middle Eastern culture, taking proper care of one's guests remains a serious obligation. To be perceived as a poor host is to be disgraced.

Jesus came into this home on perhaps the most important occasion ever held there and employed God's power to prevent two innocent young people from having to begin their married life on a sour note. By His very presence there He gave His blessing to marriage and the celebration of romantic love and lifetime commitment.

In the process He rewarded His mother's faith. And He showed His disciples that even the physical laws of nature would give way to His will, and that much, much greater adventure lay ahead for those who would trust—and, because of that trust, follow.

I think we can learn a still deeper lesson from this episode. True enough, what He did had a significant impact on the bridal couple and their families, but beyond that, what does Jesus say to us by His intervention in a matter that was clearly not one of life or death? Later He would go on to heal and save lives in danger, cast out demons, feed thousands with little, even raise the dead. Why would He begin a ministry studded with so many life-changing miracles by benefiting so few who had encountered a problem they could have survived with only embarrassment?

I think it means that our feelings matter to Him—that even on social occasions that may be important only to us, He is there, ready to help. Nervous about a first date? He doesn't want it to be awkward. Going on a job interview? He desires that you look your best. Making a speech to a large audience, but you have little public speaking experience? He would like you to appear confident and feel confident.

The twenty-first-century disciple of Jesus has a special privilege that other teens can only wish for. Whatever the issue may be, if it's important to you it's important to Him, too. Nothing is too small to deserve His notice.

The miracle at Cana would never be singled out as the most important. Usually we remember it just because it was the first, and because it was unique. But in its very uniqueness is its essence. Jesus cares about the little things. He cares about the little people.

After all, we spend most of our days, most of our lives, on the little things. Yes, the big things do come along, and if we have warning we brace for them. But in the meantime, if we have cultivated closeness with the Jesus who sees us through the little things, the big things won't seem so scary. When we know exactly which direction to look to spot Jesus in the daily routine, it isn't necessary to spend valuable time frantically searching for Him when the crisis arrives.

Jesus came to save us from our sins and to open the way for us to live forever, just as He had intended from the very beginning. But at Cana that evening He took a moment to show that He cares for our happiness now, in this life.

I don't know what your equivalent of the Cana experience will be. But I do know that the newly married couple and their embarrassed parents were no more important to Him than you are. Next time you face a problem that seems desperate to you, but relatively insignificant to everyone else, think of a night in Cana.

chapter 3

The Paralyzed Man and His Friends

A *day spent with Jesus during the first weeks of His work usually produced in us a state of sensory overload. At times it was just so overwhelming! Everywhere we turned, people were running toward us. Some were pleading, others demanding, but no matter what kind of manners they displayed, they all wanted a few moments of Jesus' attention. Something they coveted even more were the occasions Jesus would pause and detour in the direction of a specific house, stepping across the threshold of those always-open doors into private homes that suddenly were no longer so private. For many generations those families will hand down the story of the day Jesus came to "our house."*

It was on one of these afternoons during that first month or so that we found ourselves in the Capernaum household of the Jalaevs, jammed into the front room, which was barely large enough for each family member to have a seat. Jesus was in the midst of earnest conversation with the eldest Jalaev son when, suddenly, dust and large fragments of dried mud began falling on His head! Naturally, everyone looked up, and sure enough, whole portions of the roof were crumbling down on us.

We knew the house wasn't collapsing, because we could see several hands pawing through the mud plaster between the wooden beams that supported it. Clearly, a group of people, frustrated by their inability to get inside, had gone up to the roof and were systematically opening a peephole of sorts through which they could see and hear Jesus.

The Jalaevs were becoming annoyed, not so much about the damage to their home, which they could easily and quickly repair, but by the rude interruption. Someone was trying to disrupt their personal audience with Jesus—and taking advantage of their hospitality in the process!

But Jesus remained calm. As we watched the hole grow bigger, He seemed to be smiling ever so slightly. Did He, I wondered, find this amusing? All of us had edged aside to get away from the cascading dirt, but we didn't have much room to maneuver in that tightly packed house, and debris continued to pelt our clothes and faces. Larger and larger the opening grew. More and more irritated the Jalaevs became. But the expression on Jesus' face didn't change.

Then to our amazement, a sleeping mat, secured at each corner by ropes, appeared at the opening and started to descend into the room. Slowly, carefully, men were lowering another man from the roof right down at the feet of Jesus.

What nerve! All of us, including the Jalaevs, were surprised into silence.

As the mat came to rest in front of us we saw that its occupant was motionless, arms and legs twisted into a grotesque splayed position. His muscle mass seemed to have melted away to nothing. Unaccustomed to being the center of attention, he nonetheless looked up at Jesus with the most desperate eyes. Obviously he had come, as had so many others, to be healed. But you know, I don't remember that he actually said

24

anything. The man made no long spiel about how needy he was. His condition spoke rather well for itself.

Looking just once into those desperate eyes, Jesus reached down and took the man's hand. "Your sins are forgiven. Get up, take your bed, and return home."

I thought for a second that I heard a snicker from across the crowded room. If so, it never had a chance to spread. Hardly had Jesus' words registered with the young man before he stirred those wasted muscles and slowly, carefully, turned over onto his hands and knees and pushed himself up to a standing position right in front of us.

Bedlam erupted as he looked himself over and began to flex first one arm, then the other; one leg, then the other. He turned his head from side to side, bent over at the waist, and stood erect again. Now he was as limber as he had been stiff before!

That did it. Our stay in the Jalaev home had come to an abrupt end. In the midst of the rejoicing and other noise and commotion going on we excused ourselves and started down the street. But along with us came the representatives of the Pharisees, who had begun watching Jesus' every move. What they had seen had not pleased them. Their disapproval was very obvious as they hurried to Jesus' side.

"How is it that you presume to forgive sins? Only God has the authority to do that!" they fairly shouted.

Patiently Jesus replied, "You saw what I did. Which would have been easier—to forgive his sins or to command him to get up and walk?"

The Pharisees were fond of teaching that physical ailments were the direct result of one's sins. In other words, according to them, the sick really were only suffering what they deserved. It was punishment from God. Such guilt allowed them to shift the focus away from their own completely ineffective ministry. Now, with their very own eyes, they had seen Jesus heal physical affliction, and unless their own teachings were dead wrong, it meant that He could and did forgive sins. It was more than they could handle, and they melted away into the crowd.

As we came to understand from our time with Jesus, the man's disease had had nothing whatever to do with any wrongdoing on his part. It may have been something that ran in his family. Whatever it was, it had no power in the presence of the One who had come to seek and save. And whatever his condition was, Jesus swept it away, because the man and his friends had faith and were willing to do anything to bring him to Jesus.

Again and again we would hear Jesus refer to that faith. "Your faith is what has made you whole," He would say to this lame woman or that old man. "You believe in Me, so this is what I want to do for you." The ones who held nothing back, who laid themselves on the line in demonstrating their belief, never found themselves turned away.

"All it takes," He would say, "is faith the size of a mustard seed. I ask only that you believe."

Oh, they were diabolical, those Pharisees were. Isn't it amazing the places that spiritual blindness can lead otherwise good people? The corruptness of the system they had crafted reminds me a little of the corrosion that coats battery terminals when we're not careful to maintain a clean connection. The Pharisees' attitude just built up and built up to the point where they no doubt believed their own PR.

Lacking any other plausible explanation, they certainly found it convenient to their purposes to go about blaming the ill fortunes of the ordinary people on their own sinfulness. If we don't understand an affliction, blame the victim. Who's going to argue, anyway?

Meanwhile, nobody paid any attention to the complete breakdown in the relationship between the Jewish leaders—leaders of God's own chosen people—and God Himself, who would have lovingly, faithfully kept His people, including their leaders, close to Him if they had only chosen that path.

And consistent with the natural tendencies of powerful organizations, the Sanhedrin and others in the ruling class were always vigilant, watching for perceived threats to their authority. They had no provision for dealing with a traveling teacher, trained as a carpenter, who went about drawing attention to Himself and fulfilling prophecy before their very eyes. So the Pharisees' role in this story is completely in character and true to form, and they played it well. But it isn't the central role. They don't get top billing in this little drama.

In fact, I don't think I would even assign the role of the hero to the paralyzed man. True, he came to Jesus in absolute faith, and Jesus rewarded that faith. And no doubt, for the rest of his life he was a walking testimony to God's healing power.

But my nomination for heroes of this story goes to the friends. They were willing to stop at nothing to get this man to the One they believed could help him. More than that, they didn't mind looking foolish and risking arrest for damaging the Jalaevs' home. The men had to get him to Jesus. If they could place him in front of the Master, these other problems would resolve themselves.

On a scale of 1 to 10 I suspect most teens would rate their friends at 15! You may have several layers of friends, separate but interlocking groups of friends, or friends who appear within your inner circle, drift away for a time, then reappear. Typically, no matter how many friends you claim, there are two or three you consider your "best friends"—the ones you would trust with anything anytime. The ones you turn to when everything in your life is falling apart and who know all those things about you that maybe not even your parents do. They are the ones with whom you are free to be *real*.

Working with teens every day gives me some intriguing glimpses into the way they make choices and the priorities that drive their lives. They know that my generation is watching them, but they often dismiss us as merely bewildered by them, or perhaps just waiting to catch them using poor judgment so we can "take the lecture stage" and straighten them out. As a result, they don't realize how much fun they are to observe and how interested we really are in how they think.

In planning this book, I asked a lot of academy students (and some who had recently graduated) what issues affected them the most during that scary and unpredictable journey from freshman to sophomore to junior to senior. I wondered what factors were the best predictors of how successful that journey would be. Perhaps it might be the parents and home from which they came every morning, or maybe how they felt about themselves. And sure enough, those do show up as extremely important in the overall picture.

But an e-mail from one of my recent students who is now at a public university really caught my attention. "Developing friendships and defining relationships has probably been the single most difficult struggle in my teenage years," he said. "I think I easily could have ended up in a completely different position if I had met the wrong people my freshman year of academy. I was probably foolish enough to do just about anything to feel accepted and appreciated. Thankfully, the friends I made turned out halfway decent. It shouldn't have all happened by chance, though."

Friends. I can never read that e-mail without remembering the day that young man graduated from academy. The commencement ceremonies were well under way when suddenly everything stopped, and in a dramatic surprise, the doors to the baptistry opened, and there he stood in a blue robe, ready to submerge his life in commitment to Christ. It was an emotional moment, and I have never seen another one like it, before or since. He credits his friends.

As he implies in the e-mail, though, it was not a guaranteed outcome by any means. And we adults who walk the halls of Adventist high schools semester in and semester out know it all too well. We see the little knots of kids in the parking lot and hear about the parties, the risky car rides, the shoplifting expeditions to see who can pick up the most loot without arousing suspicion, the laughter about clueless parents. While we may not know exactly when and where, we know the alcohol flows, and we witness the results. Sometimes we get asked to help put the pieces back together. At that point, the "friends" have often moved on.

Also we see the prayer and Bible study groups formed, the money being saved for mission trips, the kids who tutor their peers in math and physics, the young men and women who assume leadership roles in community projects. Often we can identify early on the teens who are going to leave their mark on a school long after they have graduated.

Truthfully, I have known only a couple of students who moved easily and comfortably in and out of the two contrasting groups, universally popular, enjoying the confidence of both. I don't think they were cynically playing each group off against the other. They were, I believe, sincere in assuming that they could have it both ways. Each of them had the remarkable and almost unique gift of seeming to fit in with both the hell-raisers and the holy Joes. So why not? Well . . .

I sit at my keyboard and easily call to mind their faces. Coincidentally, they had the same first name. They also share the same predicament these days—thrashing about, searching to discover who they really are. As they leave their academy peer groups behind and progress into young adulthood, neither of them claims a close relationship with Jesus, and neither boasts nearly the same universal popularity they once obviously had. Now they wander into the future, uncertain of their destinations, unable to identify what they have to show for the years they spent in a Christ-centered environment.

Until the day we notice water running uphill, we will continue to see teens influence each other without even trying. It is in the nature of the way God made us. What a gift we have—to be able to surround a friend in trouble and do whatever it takes to bring them to the One who can answer all his questions, meet all her needs!

How many roofs have you dismantled lately to get to Jesus with someone who needs Him?

chapter 4

A Sabbath
Meal

Remember the sabbath day, to keep it holy. Six days shalt thou labour, and do all thy work: but the seventh day is the sabbath of the Lord thy God: in it thou shalt not do any work, thou, nor thy son, nor thy daughter . . ."

James and I had grown up with these words carved upon our hearts. The law of God was the code of the Zebedee household. Zebedee boats and their crews were never on the lake on the Sabbath. Nor were Zebedee fish ever en route to the markets in Jerusalem and other parts of Palestine on the Sabbath. Never. Most of the other disciples came from similar backgrounds of observing the law. This was life-and-death stuff. You didn't mess with the Sabbath.

Not that it was a burden to our family. On the contrary, in our home the Sabbath was always such a welcome contrast to the other six days. True, our weekly trip to the synagogue for worship was not always as spiritually rewarding as God might have wished for us. But that was all right, because we didn't observe the Sabbath in order to hear deep revelations about God from the rabbis. We did it because He *had ordered it and it was the right thing to do. The Lord rested on the seventh day of Creation week and hallowed it—we rested on the seventh day of every week and savored it. Who wouldn't appreciate a day free of muscle strains, blisters, and repairing torn nets and leaky boats?*

Only gradually did the realization dawn on our little band of Jesus' fellow travelers that after lives spent so far observing the Sabbath as a requirement, we were now spending the Sabbath . . . with the Lord of the Sabbath!

Weekly we passed 24 hours of sacred time in the presence of the very One who had begun it so many centuries ago—the very One who understood the Sabbath as none of us ever had. Those hours would ultimately color our consciousness of the Sabbath for as long as we would live, and, we hoped, would be the experience of all to whom we would pass on that gift.

You must understand that Jesus talked about His Father in heaven a lot. Scarcely a day would go by without some mention of Their crucial relationship. But on the Sabbath those conversations with the Father—and with us about the Father—went on hour after hour. And we never tired of them!

It was something like a guided tour of the kingdom, provided by the crown prince Himself. Every week, without fail, we learned something new about the world, the universe, the forces of love that whisper themselves into every person's breath, that inhabit every singing bird, every gust of wind, every stalk of grain. Every week Jesus showed us a brand-new dimension of the Father, gave us a fresh look at heaven. And every Sabbath He opened a new installment in the contest between good and evil—the contest of kingdoms, I called it—and we saw behind the curtains into the shadows where God waits to reclaim those who love Him.

So on this day that brought us closest to God, it was ironic that our innocent fellowship would hurl us back to the center of God's heartache—counterfeit truth.

We were so wrapped up in Jesus' stories that we never saw them coming. Pharisees. A whole squadron of them. Embarrassment at failing to defeat Jesus in argument had forced them to travel in little packs so that if one of them couldn't think of a way to entrap Him with His own words, perhaps another could.

Strolling serenely down a pathway between two grainfields, we were idly reaching over to pluck off some grain here and there to eat as we walked. It was all perfectly legal, of course. Travelers in Palestine were always welcome to help themselves to a farmer's standing grain as long as we didn't get out the heavy equipment and start harvesting it on a wholesale basis. Grazing randomly through someone's fields or orchards, as we were doing, wasn't theft—it was availing ourselves of normal hospitality. But remember . . . this was the Sabbath.

Without warning, a chilly, rasping voice came from several yards behind us. "Why are you doing what is illegal on the Sabbath?"

Thinking back on that Sabbath afternoon after many decades of Sabbaths since it happened, I am filled only with pity at the smallness and ignorance of anyone who would have the audacity to question the Lord of the Sabbath about how He was using His day! I can never forget the look on Jesus' face as He turned to His accuser.

"Are you forgetting David?" He asked. "You call David a great man, and you've honored him for centuries along with your other ancestors. Yet he took the sacred bread from the tabernacle, bread meant only for the priests."

It had happened again!

Momentarily stung by this surprise example of God's symbols tak-

ing less importance than human need, the Pharisees were silent. They looked at each other, muttering quietly, "You answer Him." "No, you answer Him!"

It would have been comical if it hadn't been so important a moment.

Jesus plunged ahead into the opening. "The Sabbath was made for humanity, not humanity for the Sabbath. The Son of man is Lord of the Sabbath." And with that, He led us calmly on past the rows of grain, picking up where He had left off in His narrative about the Father.

Reasoning that perseverance would render better opportunities for entrapment, the group of Pharisees stuck with us as we walked back into town toward the synagogue. Sure enough, they hadn't finished with Jesus quite yet.

Spotting a man with a deformed hand, they challenged Jesus. "Is it lawful to heal on the Sabbath?"

This time the scorn in His face was hard to miss as He wheeled on the speaker and demanded, "Which of you would allow a fallen sheep of yours to remain lying in a pit on the Sabbath? Is not this man more important than a sheep?"

With that, He called to the man to come forward and stretch out his hand, and at that very moment it was healed to perfection.

We saw no more of the Pharisees that day. But now the line had been drawn. The religious leaders had destroyed the bridge across which they could have crossed the gulf separating them from truth. Their course was set.

They're still at it today. The Pharisees, I mean. Of course, there wouldn't be any in your church congregation. Not a chance!

Mine either. But trust me, they're out there. If you're looking for the bearded guys in robes like the ones you've seen in the illustrations to Arthur Maxwell's *Bible Story,* forget it. That was then. This is now. They wear suits. Men's *and* women's suits. And they hang out in the strangest places!

I once knew one whose post of duty was the women's room at church. It was the perfect spot to pull aside young women and give them all the reasons their makeup detracted from their witness. (You think I'm making that up? Uh-uh. True story.) Fortunately, the congregation did not allow her "ministry" to continue for long.

Our denominational struggle with pharisaism is not new. It just evolves with the passing of time, taking different forms, pursuing different agendas. But its characteristics hark back to the original Pharisees of 20 centuries ago. We're not talking about evil people. In fact, we're discussing the saints—people who are absolutely convinced they are doing the Lord's work. And believe it or not, sometimes they are!

That's the complicated part. Just as in Jesus' day, much of what they embrace as truth is indeed truth—important truth. God does hold His people to a higher standard. He does expect us to stand apart from the world's values. And He does want us to keep the Sabbath holy and to honor the other commandments as well. What we, who claim to be God's people, do *does* matter.

The problem creeps in when we allow the values of the kingdom of God, which run as a consistent theme throughout the Bible, to become arbitrary commands that we must observe just because they are the rules. Jesus plainly told the religious authorities of His day, whose Sabbath observance was driven solely by their compulsion to carry out the letter of the law, "You don't know what you're doing, and you've forgotten why you're doing it."

So why do we keep the Sabbath holy? What exactly was God's purpose in setting that day apart from the rest and asking us to behave differently during that particular 24-hour period?

Think of the opportunity John and the other disciples had, to spend three years' worth of Sabbaths in the company of the One who had conceived and established it!

Don't think that they didn't notice that Jesus completely ignored the arbitrary, burdensome rules governing how far one could travel on the Sabbath and how heavy one's cargo could be. We have no record of Jesus ever taking part in the ridiculous custom of pinning some item from home on His garment so that He could claim He hadn't actually left His "home." Some Jews really did this!

Also, they were not to cook or even light a fire. I'm reminded of the observance of some Jews in our own time—again, well-meaning people who believe they are honoring God. Once I stayed over Sabbath in a four-star hotel in Jerusalem. The coffee shop remained open on the Sabbath, but the only hot item on the menu was coffee, kept hot by a flame carefully lit before the Sabbath began!

Entering the hotel elevator, I encountered a sad-eyed Jewish boy about 15 years old. His job was to ride up and down all Friday evening (he was back in the morning!), spending *his* Sabbath in that claustrophobic environment with special permission to push the buttons for each floor, thus sparing others the necessity of using electricity on the Sabbath. During the years since I've wondered if that poor young man ever came to call the Sabbath a delight.

God doesn't laugh about this. And I think He doesn't laugh about *our* serious philosophical discussions about what is or is not acceptable Sabbath activity. Debates about playing catch in the driveway, eating out in a restaurant, or renting canoes to go downriver are not what He intended for His people at all. Not even close!

I believe God wants His young disciples in the twenty-first century to be so closely tied to Him and His kingdom that they will intuitively understand how to keep a day holy, spending it in His presence, remembering His supreme acts of love in creating us, sustaining us, redeeming us, and promising to return for us. And what if you and I, in the privacy of our own families and our own consciences, come to somewhat different conclusions about the activities we find appropriate?

If you suspect me of discounting the importance of the Sabbath, you misunderstand. Quite the contrary. I have observed the Sabbath my whole life and raised my children to do the same. I would never have done that if I thought it unimportant. In my experience, God knew precisely what was best for us and created this special day, not just so we would remember His work of Creation, but for the benefit of our physical and spiritual welfare as well.

I believe that God calls His twenty-first-century disciples to know Him so well, to take so much delight in spending time with Him, that we will have no interest in judging the details of others' Sabbath observance. Jesus said it Himself: We were not made to adhere to strict rules about the number of minutes until "holy time" is over. He created the Sabbath for us, drawing us into His presence, giving us time to practice living with Him in eternity, filling us with better understanding of how much He loves us and wants us to relate to Him.

When you see the sun setting at the end of another Sabbath, imagine the voice of Jesus speaking to you softly, individually, "Thank you for this time. I am with you always, but I feel honored that you chose to be with Me today. Let's do it again next week. Come back to Me, and we will rest together."

It is the way of a disciple's life. We do it not because others will think less of us if we don't follow a custom, and not because it's a rule. Rather, we do it because we were *created* to do it. Each week we celebrate the Sabbath because the Lord of our lives is also the Lord of the Sabbath. It runs in the family.

chapter 5

The Storm on the Lake

When I think of those days with Jesus, certain scenes instantly pop into my mind. Nearly every day had some truly remarkable event, some experience that I had never had before. Our lives moved rapidly from one adventure to another—so radically different from the predictable days and nights on the lake I had always known—and I remember periods when all of us were just exhausted. Dealing with hundreds of people who all wanted something from the Master took a toll on us. Jesus recognized the signs of fatigue, and from time to time He made it a point to take us away from the clamoring mobs and just let us spend an evening together as a group of friends.

One evening He could tell we had had enough. And He was pretty tired Himself. James and I had arranged to have one of the Zebedee boats tied up near where Jesus had been teaching along the shore. To our delight, He welcomed the chance to escape the crowd and sail to the other side of the lake. He knew that people would eventually find us, but meanwhile we could have a little downtime.

In spite of our weariness, we were in high spirits that night. The moon had risen, obscured at times by scudding clouds, and as we shared *our supper we enjoyed the gentle rocking of the boat. Mellow evenings like this—pleasant surroundings, intimate friends—make the best memories. I found myself nestled in the stern, facing the moon and its star-dusted backdrop, listening to Jesus tell stories. He recounted incidents from the carpenter shop in Nazareth, stories of His earliest memories as a child in Egypt—He had actually seen the pyramids!*

But, as always on such occasions, He talked about Himself only in response to our questions. Even then, He always found an opportunity to channel the conversation to the future, to His kingdom, and to His Father. Always He told us something about God that we would never have otherwise known. It was a sweet, sweet time. But after an hour or so, it was obvious that Jesus Himself needed sleep. Later, when I glanced His way, I saw that His eyes were closed.

Heaven seemed very near to us that night. As I think about it now, I'm sure there must have been a steady stream of angels coming and going between the Father's throne room and our little boat, delivering fresh supplies of inspiration, energy, and assurance that Jesus' connection to that other realm was fully alive and very real. Had we been able to see all that heavenly traffic, perhaps the event that would soon overtake us would not have been so terrifying. If we could have had the mind of Jesus, resting serenely in His Father's love and care, we might have met the coming storm differently.

I have forgotten how long I too slept. All I remember is the sudden sharp pain from being struck on the side of my face by a steering oar as Judas lost control of the boat.

For a moment it felt as though the blow had broken my cheekbone, but I didn't really have time to focus on that, because we were clearly in big trouble. Wave after wave came crashing across the bow. Each time we plunged into the trough that followed there was a good chance the next wave would be the end. With the wind shrieking so loudly I could barely hear the voices of my friends shouting instructions to each other. I realized I was soaked to the skin. It was hard to tell whether I was so wet because of the water splashing over the side or the rain pelting down. It didn't matter.

Andrew and Peter were bailing as fast as they could. Judas and James struggled to hang on to the wildly swinging steering oar. The others were grabbing everything they could to throw overboard. How could this have happened? Most of us were experienced sailors. It wasn't like us to be caught unprepared by a storm. Nor was it like us to be this afraid. But yes, we were very terrified.

My mind raced. It must have been just like this the night the Ben-Hovums' boat capsized with all hands lost. Their last moments would have been exactly like this!

I imagined my mother walking in a procession to the graveyard.

A telltale cracking noise from above warned us that the mainsail was threatening to give way. It was the unmistakable sound of disaster.

At that exact moment—finally someone remembered Jesus, and realized that He wasn't helping to save the boat. Hearing someone shout His name, I looked at the spot where I had last seen Him resting. Sure enough, His feet were sticking out from beneath a tarp that the gale-force wind had flung over Him. He wasn't moving. My first thought was that flying debris might have hurt Him, but as we rushed over to Him to rouse Him, He sat up and looked around. He was obviously fine.

Jesus had been deep in His fatigue-induced sleep, completely unaware of our danger.

"How can You do this to us, Master?" *Thaddaeus yelled.* "We're about to go down! Don't You even care?"

It's hard to re-create the scene with only words. Our situation was

41

truly desperate, with water cascading over the bow every time we hit the bottom of a trough. The incredible wind blocked out most other sounds. We scrambled around to grab anything that we could throw overboard while at the same time trying to stay inside the boat ourselves.

We pulled Jesus to His feet just as the boat lurched. For a second I thought we were all going over the side. Blindly I thrust out my hand to grab the nearest object. It was Jesus' right arm—the same arm I had just been pulling on. Only now He was standing still and upright!

"Peace! Be still!" He said.

The wind ceased immediately, and with that the waves calmed down. Within a minute or so the surface of the lake was placid and smooth.

"Where was your faith?" Jesus inquired. "Why were you so fearful?"

No one rushed to answer. It was a moment that combined relief at our narrow escape, weariness from the hard work of keeping the boat right side up, and extreme embarrassment that, for a time, we had forgotten that Jesus was there!

We were becoming accustomed to watching Him do miraculous things, but the display of power over the forces of nature was so astonishing that we hardly knew how to react. "What kind of man is this?" some of the others muttered under their breath. But even as they asked, they really knew. In Scripture one person alone rebuked or commanded the sea—the Lord God Himself.

On any Tuesday morning (make it a Wednesday, if you prefer) you can stand in the hallway of any high school or academy between periods and watch the little vignettes unfold, quick two-minute dramas, complete with starring roles, supporting players, and often, multilayered story lines. Except these dramas are usually not scripted and produced for an audience. They are quite real. The actors are not paid to perform—in many cases they would give anything to be in a different play altogether.

Comparing the daily life of a twenty-first-century teen to a play is not to trivialize or poke fun in any way. Progressing through adolescence into adulthood has never been easy, but in recent decades we have seen it become a much more intense and risky process. Often the adult characters in these plays are complicating factors. They don't *mean* to be—mostly they just are.

If your drama has strong comedic overtones, rejoice! Several good laughs every day are therapeutic. Maybe your drama is a romance or an adventure, leading you from one thrilling and daring exploit to another, a series of unpredictable and often rewarding episodes full of deeper meaning.

But some of these dramas are true horror stories. Faculty members understand (even though we receive precious little credit for this) that on any given day in a large school, literally dozens of students walk through the door in various stages of emotional disarray. When I say that "faculty members understand," I mean, of course, that we know the odds and we can draw on our experience with hundreds or thousands of other teens. We may not know, just by encountering you in the parking lot, the exact environment you came from when you left your driveway 20 minutes ago.

For example, we may not intuitively understand that you have just returned from a long car trip with your mother, during which she repeatedly berated you with such award-winning lines as "It would have been better if you'd never been born! Everything in my life has been downhill since."

Nor may we know that you've just been told your parents are splitting up. We may not have anticipated, as you have all weekend, that you're about to be dumped flat by your significant other, or that your dad is about to lose his job, or that you think you just may have cancer.

43

Unless it happens to be our subject, we may not be aware of how desperately you are struggling to pass geometry or precalculus. We may be oblivious to your angst over being cut from the cross-country team or the select choir. If you wanted to run for class treasurer, only to discover that your best friend already has plans to do exactly that (she just never bothered to tell you), we can't divine that out of thin air.

But often those of us who pay attention (yes, some of us do) can spot a troubled kid, even if we don't know exactly what's going on in his or her life. We wish you would trust us more. Perhaps some of us haven't earned your trust. Despite that, we still invite you to take a chance on us.

Are there exceptions? Of course. We could all name a few. But for the most part, the teachers you find in a high school, especially in an Adventist academy, are there because they felt pulled toward working with—well, people just *like* you. Teenagers, believe it or not. We actually *like* you—well, most of you. We go to work every day out of the conviction that what we do is critically important, and we do understand that helping you master the intricacies of proofs and theorems and teaching you how a bill becomes a law are only a part of our jobs. The other part is to care about you. The quality of your life actually matters to us. Do you believe that?

We are there to care and to mentor. But mostly we are there to point you toward the One who can do far more than that. It would have mattered little if Jesus had awakened in that fear-filled boat, wrung His hands, and said, "Wow, fellows, this looks like real trouble! How can I help?" What if He had grabbed another bucket and started bailing like everyone else?

But those frantic men discovered that when you're in the presence of the Creator of the universe, a storm is no match for Him. He has the power. Today's teens, whose problems can be very real and very troubling, often make the mistake of overlooking a solution that is hiding in plain sight. Whenever a student in an

Adventist school manages to muddle through an entire day in our classes and study halls and chapels without catching at least a glimpse of Jesus and His amazing power to change their lives, we have failed. No student should ever drive away from an Adventist school with a hopeless feeling in their heart, afraid of what the evening might bring.

To believe the gospel account of Jesus as He stands in that out-of-control boat and calmly commands the wind and the waves to be still is to believe that whatever is out of control in our lives is well within His sovereign reach as well.

It's a struggle out there, guys. We know. And we realize that it's far more intense for you than it was for us. The good news is that He knows too. If you have trust issues because some friend or an adult in your life has betrayed you, what do you have to lose by trusting Jesus?

"I will never leave you nor forsake you," He said. Did He really mean that? John and James and Matthew and Peter and all the others discovered that He did. As we will see, the final testimony of John's life affirms it.

If you have a particularly painful or scary challenge in your life right now, I invite you to see for yourself what Jesus will do with it. He waits for you to trust Him with it and to discover that He already has a plan to deal with it.

chapter 6

Jairus

Sorting through the memories of those days with Jesus, I find certain faces coming to mind more often than others. We witnessed so many phenomenal things within such a short period of time, and each miraculous incident has its own place in my memories. I can picture each scene, even tell you what the weather was like. But some of the faces . . .

Jairus's is one of them. Even now, many years later, when I feel a certain mood, I see his face as he ran up to the Master.

It was never a warming experience to see Jairus. He was part of the local Jewish synagogue establishment—not really a priest or rabbi, more an administrator. We knew well how that whole crowd felt about Jesus. They didn't try to hide their contempt. So to see him rushing up to us soon after we landed back on the western shore of the lake was actually somewhat annoying. Then I got a good look at his expression. It was an anguished face as he looked up pleadingly at Jesus from about knee level, where he had suddenly knelt and grasped the Master's legs.

"My little daughter is lying at death's door," he wailed. "Come *and lay Your hands on her, that she may be cured and live."*

Immediately Jesus followed, as Jairus seized Him by the wrist and elbow and swept Him away in the direction of his home. It all happened so quickly that we didn't have much time to piece together what had really taken place. Certainly the circumstances must have been serious to change Jairus's attitude so radically and so quickly. What must have been at stake for him to swallow so much pride, risk so much status, and be willing to humbly request help from someone he despised?

We had seen Jesus speak with the religious authorities before, and often He was very blunt with them. He didn't hesitate to point out their hypocrisy, the futility of their rituals, their spiritual bankruptcy. For an instant we wondered why He had skipped the lecture this time.

The people who had greeted us at the lakeshore swelled in number almost exponentially as our little procession hurried along. Soon, as usually happened when word spread that Jesus was nearby, the road became clogged with well-wishers, pitiable and poverty-stricken people begging for help or healing, and, of course, the plague of hangers-on, those who weren't entirely sure what was happening but wanted to share the excitement anyway. It made for really slow going.

Suddenly, in the midst of all that pushing and shoving, Jesus stiffened. He stopped in His tracks and quickly looked around in every direction.

"Who touched Me?" He asked.

Thinking that He was being funny, I started to chuckle. In retrospect I now realize that joking in that manner wouldn't have been consistent with the way He normally used humor. He wasn't laughing. In fact, He wasn't even smiling. And He had stopped in His tracks. The thought crossed my mind that perhaps He wouldn't move on until He figured out whatever had happened.

The woman had been cowering about 15 feet away, her face mostly covered. But when she realized that Jesus really did want to see her, she resigned herself to stepping forward. In a moment we heard her whole story. She had been ill for 12 years and had mostly given up ever being healed. Of course she had heard what Jesus was doing for people everywhere He went. But how could she stand to be so conspicuous? She didn't want to be a spectacle. Twelve long years of being "different" had been quite enough. The woman had no appetite for being on display.

But oh, the thought of being healed, of having this curse lifted! While she was willing to risk exposure, if need be, she truly believed that if she merely touched Him and ran away, it would be enough.

And you know, it would have been. For in that instant as she made contact with the hem of His robe, she was healed. It actually would not have been necessary for her to come forward and identify herself. But it was not enough for Jesus. He wanted to see her, to know her. Jesus desired to understand the need of the one who trusted Him this much. And He wanted to tell her that it was her belief itself that had healed her.

It was a very moving moment. Years of suffering erased by a simple touch—and not Jesus' touch, at that! Rather, it was her touching of Him.

But we dared not linger over this woman. Her need had been met. A more urgent one waited at Jairus's home.

But just as we resumed our mission a grim-faced messenger met us. The young man seemed clearly troubled by what he had to tell Jairus. He tried to be tactful, but there are only so many ways to tell a man that his little girl has died. "Don't trouble the teacher anymore," he suggested, trying to be helpful.

A respectful hush fell over the part of the crowd closest to us. No one was sure what to say. Except Jesus.

"Don't be afraid," He said, looking right into Jairus's eyes. "Just keep believing."

Turning around to our group, He singled out Peter and James and me to accompany Him and asked the others to remain behind. On we trudged, with much less urgency now, to the home where death had just called.

We heard the wailing several blocks away. The professional mourners, sensing an imminent opportunity, had apparently been standing by, anticipating their employment. So they wasted no time before the loud lament began rising over the neighborhood, and all were aware that Jairus's daughter—the lovely 12-year-old light of his life—had died.

The atmosphere was oppressive as we crossed the threshold into that house of fresh grief. A sense of mourning filled it everywhere, the genuine mingling with the artificial and mercenary. What family is prepared to lose a child? This one was devastated.

I watched Jesus' face as He surveyed the scene. His reflected sorrow as well. Gently He asked the paid mourners and even most of the family members to step outside. Then, putting His arm around the girl's mother, He said, "Take Me to her."

Six of us entered the bedchamber silently—Jesus, the parents, Peter, James, and me. The girl looked so small. So pale.

In silence Jesus approached the bedside and reached for her hand.

"Young woman, I say to you, rise."

The eyelids fluttered, she coughed a couple of times, and then, as though it were any other morning, she threw back the bedcovers and swung her feet off her sleeping mat.

The parents exploded with joy! Alongside that anguished father's face just an hour or so earlier, I keep in my memory the next two minutes in that small bedroom as the mother and father grabbed that little girl and embraced her.

I need not describe the commotion in the rest of the household when they realized what had happened. Jesus cautioned them not to tell about it, but how could they not? This girl who had been claimed by death had now been returned to them by a loving God who clearly had ultimate power over death. It was not something to keep quiet about.

The harassment from the synagogue where Jairus served stopped as of that day. Jesus had given him a glimpse inside the kingdom of God that years of managing a house of worship could never have offered him. This was a God to whom people and their sorrows were far more important than forms and spiritually bankrupt rituals. He understood now—he really understood.

Death is not just for the old. In my junior English classes we discover that it is a subject that has fascinated poets and storytellers for centuries. Sometimes even the writer is quite young. William Cullen Bryant wrote "Thanatopsis," a brilliant meditation on death, when he was 17, revealing uncommon insight into human nature for someone his age.

But most kids don't have Bryant's perspective. As an academy teacher I have observed teenagers coping with the unexpected loss of a friend, and usually they are completely unprepared. We just don't think of death as a prospect for anyone but those who have "lived a full life" and are in their declining years. When Grandma dies, we are saddened. Remembering fondly the wonderful times we had at her house, we look forward to seeing her again when Jesus comes the second time. But we are not shocked at her death.

It's a different story when Jared, the kid who sat next to you in Algebra II, gets killed on the way home from school. After the initial disbelief, we usually go into an anger stage: angry at ourselves, perhaps, because Jared had asked us for a favor and we never got around to doing it—and angry at God. Why would a loving God allow it to happen?

If you've been there, you know what I mean. My first experience with this involved a friend with whom I had gone to school as an academy freshman. When we became sophomores, he decided to go to a boarding school several hundred miles away. On the way back to school after Thanksgiving break that fall, his car went off the road, killing him.

Just a few years later, on a rainy spring day, I sat behind two other friends in my college psychology class. They were late to class that day. They came in together, umbrellas dripping and slightly embarrassed, unburdened themselves of their piles of books, and sat down in front of me. But they were smiling. I remember that. I never found out why they were late, because I never saw them again. That evening, on the way back from an expedition to town, they collided with another car. Today, almost 34 years later, one of them lies in a cemetery just two miles from where I write these lines.

So I have experienced the kind of loss you as a teen have probably had. It does get your attention. And it does focus your mind—for a while.

But when I think of Jesus' encounter with Jairus and his daughter, I bring a different frame of reference to the story. I have been Jairus.

My daughter was older than his—twice as old. But still, 24 is young by anyone's standards. And our stories differed in other ways. Instead of hired mourners standing by, just waiting to swing into action with their dramatic wails, we had literally dozens of Karen's friends crowded into her hospital room, reading Bible texts, singing to her, praying with her. The ICU staff had never seen anything like it. For two days, around the clock, Jesus was in Karen's room just as surely as He had been in Jairus's daughter's room, but we saw Him in the presence of her dearest loved ones.

After Karen slipped away from us that beautiful fall day, her friends and other family members, having given all that they had for her, left to console each other. I stepped away as well, to gather myself and to make some necessary phone calls. A little while later I returned to her room and asked the nurse if I could be alone with her for a few moments.

The machines were off now, and the room was still. Sunlight streamed in through the window as I held her left hand and stroked her forehead for the last time. Even knowing that she didn't hear, I spoke briefly out loud, perhaps reassuring myself more than anything else of her place in my heart and my love for her that would not die.

I spoke to God, too. As I looked around the room I did not see Jesus standing there beside me. But I knew He was there, as I had known He was there all along, through the night watches, through the pain and the heroic efforts to save Karen.

I actually thought of Jairus's daughter that afternoon. She went through my mind as I stood holding Karen's hand. I didn't ask God to raise her. It was enough that I knew that He could. Karen had trusted God her whole life. My job was to continue trusting Him for her.

Jesus' ministry makes it clear that illness and death are enemies, and it's never good to be preoccupied or obsessed with the enemy. With Jairus's daughter, with the young boy in Nain, with His own friend, Lazarus, and perhaps with others of whom we don't know, Jesus showed that His power over death is complete. He gave us a peek inside His kingdom in which death will no longer be a threat. He says to us, "Look, death was never My idea, and when you trust Me, you need never fear it again."

Part of discipleship in the twenty-first century involves being fearless in the face of death. Can you pull that off? I believe you can. I've seen it done.

chapter 7

A Little Walk
on the Water

Y ou would have to know Peter to fully appreciate what happened
the night we sailed without Jesus. The day had already been
unforgettable. We had received word of the execution of John, the
cousin who had been preparing the way for Jesus' ministry. The grief,
on top of the pace Jesus had been setting for Himself (and us), was almost more than He could bear.

Jesus and John had met only once, the day Jesus asked to be bap-
tized. Still, in spite of the short time they spent together, the bond was
a close one because of the relationship of their mothers and because both
men were keenly aware of each other's role in God's plan. The realization that John's ministry, so essential to herald the arrival of the
Messiah, had now led to his death brought Jesus to the lowest point we
had witnessed in the short time we had known Him.

He needed to escape—not for His own safety so much as for time to
reflect on John's life and to talk with His own Father. But the crowds
would not leave, and as first one would ask for help or healing, then another, He felt the time slipping away. Actually, it was drawing toward

evening, and thousands of people had gathered. Whenever Jesus was in the neighborhood, word of His presence spread at amazing speed.

Looking back on this particular day, I'm still not sure how, with our limited experience, we managed to cope with everything that happened. The lateness of the hour combined with the remote location far outside the nearest town, and people in the crowd began to complain about their hunger. Few of them had brought their supper with them, and of those who had, fewer still were willing to bring it out lest they be expected to share with everyone else.

Suddenly Jesus startled us by declaring, "Give them something to eat." What? There were thousands of people here! He knew very well the food we had on hand would not even begin to satisfy the demand. To be precise, it consisted of five loaves of bread and two fish. If you figure the portions judiciously, that was just about enough to feed the 13 of us! Nonetheless, He had said it.

Cautiously we began to break up the bread and pass it around, at the same time bracing ourselves for the reaction, as many would soon realize that those closest to us had at least a snack and the rest of them did not. The response never came. As the bread and chunks of fish passed from hand to hand, each individual managed to break off enough to make him or her happy and keep the servings moving.

We had never seen anything like this! Before our eyes, this pack of selfish, whining, hungry people transformed back into a receptive congregation, their physical needs met for the time being, their minds again ready to focus on Jesus and what He had already shown them about God.

But by now He was more than ready to be alone. I had never known anyone so touched, so moved, by the pain of other people. After many hours of listening and feeling and releasing God's power into these people, He needed desperately to refill Himself by direct contact with the Father.

So He sent us away. All of us. Dismissing the crowd—not an easy task—He dispatched us to take the boat to the other side of the lake, promising to join us later.

We didn't like to leave Him like that. But the choice was not ours. He simply motioned toward the eastern shore, and the next thing we knew He was climbing the hillside by Himself.

We often speculated about what He did during those solitary inter-ludes. Sometimes He would refer to times He spent with His Father, but He never supplied any details. Occasionally we would see brief snatches of His prayer times, but when He went off into the hills, we were left to our imaginations.

Well, this was our calling now—to do whatever He asked us to do, even if the reason was not immediately clear. So as the people dispersed to their homes and Jesus disappeared into His solitude, we shoved away from shore, set the sails, and designated a couple of us to watch and steer (where, we weren't sure). The rest of us settled back to rehash the after-noon's events. As the hours passed we drifted off to sleep.

Around 3:00 a.m. we awoke to a typical Galilean storm of the kind we had been observing all our lives. Lightning crackled in the dis-tance, illuminating the choppy surf, and the rain was starting to pelt us uncomfortably. I wouldn't say it was as dangerous as the storm in which Jesus had restored calm to the elements simply by a command. But it was bad enough, and slowly but surely it pounded away at us, until we feared the worst. Then . . .

"What's that!"

Everyone heard the alarm in Andrew's voice as he pointed back toward the western shore of the lake.

At first it was hard to see through the pouring rain, but sure enough, there seemed to be someone standing about 50 yards off the stern! Whenever the lightning flashed we could see for an instant the figure of a man, but he seemed to be completely alone, and there was no boat anywhere in sight!

I think Jesus understood immediately how terrified we were, and true to the kindness of His nature, He did not keep us in suspense. This was not a practical joke to be strung out as long as possible. Right away He called out to us, "Courage! It is I. Don't be afraid!"

It is hard to sort out now which was greater—our relief that we were not being visited by a ghost, or our amazement that Jesus was truly walking across the water toward us. Later He told us that His private conversation with the Father had come to a close. Even though it was still the middle of the night, He knew that the storm was coming and that we might be fearful, so He came out just to be with us and help. This was the Jesus we were coming to know. We shouldn't have been so surprised.

Also, we shouldn't have been surprised that Peter's reaction was more dramatic than most. "Lord, if it's You, let me walk out to You!" he shouted across the water. At first we thought he was joking, but as he started toward the side of the boat, we could see in his face that he really wanted to try it. This was Peter, all right.

But nothing will silence a chorus of scornful laughter like the voice of Jesus Himself saying, "Come."

Had we heard Him right? Was this really going to happen?

Almost involuntarily a half dozen hands reached out to Peter as he swung his legs over the side of the boat, still rocking in the not-too-gentle waves. He waved them off. Jesus had invited him to walk on water, and he was going to do it! Did we really expect him to sink?

In an instant he was out of the boat. And yes, unsteady as his footing necessarily was in the rough water, clearly he was standing upright and still on the surface!

One step. Two. Three. He put some distance between himself and the boat. We knew it couldn't be momentum keeping him up—he wasn't going that fast. But as I remember the incident, still burned into my memory by the brilliant flashes of lightning, I have a clear picture of Peter, perhaps 20 feet out, walking away from us toward the Man who had called him.

Then it happened. Some would later say that knowing Peter, he had probably begun to show off. Realizing that he was doing something no one else had ever done, he could not resist the urge to glance back at us and gloat. Maybe. But I was there, and I don't think that's what happened.

I think it suddenly dawned on him that it was just a foolish stunt—that this time he had undoubtedly gone too far. He had put himself in real danger. The windblown waves were very, very real. The depth of the lake and the darkness of the night were real too. And here he was, in dire peril, between two havens he had counted on—safety in the familiar boat and safety in the grasp of Jesus. Either one he could have trusted. But suddenly he was on his own in neither place!

"Master!" he yelled. Whatever pride may have seized him he now momentarily forgot. It wasn't funny—or even fun—anymore. "Save me!"

In a heartbeat Jesus was at his side, holding him up, escorting him back to the safety of the boat. "Why did you doubt?" He asked gently.

One after another we rushed to Jesus' side to embrace Him and acknowledge that truly He was the Son of God. We had believed it before, of course, but each new incident reinforced the reality of what only weeks before would have been impossible to foresee. We were in the presence of someone, sent by God, who could literally do anything, suspending the laws of nature whenever that was necessary to demonstrate God's love.

I'm afraid it would take us some time to realize that it was the quiet times with Jesus, the occasions when He would speak of His Father and the kingdom of heaven, that held the true center of His ministry. The dramatic moments were effective in focusing our attention, but it was in the quiet truths that were always available to those close to Him that the secret of life could really be found.

It had been a very good question that Jesus asked upon entering the boat with Peter: "Why did you doubt?" I wish I could say that after that, we never doubted. The record reveals something quite different.

We've all experienced the nagging "What if?"s. I hope you haven't fallen for the myth that being afflicted by the "What if?"s is a sign of immaturity, and that arriving at adulthood will pull you out of it.

I also hope you haven't fallen for the myth that indulging in occasional rounds of the nagging "What if?"s is a sign of *spiritual* immaturity, and that if only you were a better, more dedicated Christian, such thoughts would never occur to you again.

Spiritual immaturity is a problem, of course, and large numbers of us suffer it to varying degrees, regardless of our chronological age. But before we come down too hard on Peter—and also on the other disciples, all of whom spent weeks and months and ultimately years talking to Jesus in person every day—we should just admit that entertaining doubt is part of what we do.

Do I believe that God will help me pass that geometry exam, especially if I have been conscientious about preparing for it? Well, of course I do. Does that belief eliminate the anxiety, the butterflies in my gut, as the hour of the exam approaches? Not always. Does my belief make problem 7 less of a challenge? No.

So . . . having spent time with the same Jesus who took a few pieces of bread and fish and fed thousands of people with them, the same Jesus who promised Peter that he would successfully walk across water and who plucked him to safety when his courage failed—why do we doubt?

I suppose it's because we don't often see the people around us actually walking on water—that is, doing the impossible. But our not seeing it may be the result of not knowing where to look. I believe teens are doing remarkable things like that every day.

I have seen teens make themselves responsible for an entire public evangelistic series. Often I have heard them perform difficult and demanding oratorios that would have seemed impossible only a few weeks earlier. And most of all, I have watched them reach out to each other in serious personal crisis, with the kind of support that only peers can provide.

It is unlikely that God is actually standing on the water, calling you to physically walk out to Him. Peter is the only one we know to have actually had that experience. But it is quite possible that God is preparing you for a challenge that will strike you as equally difficult to meet. How much do you trust Him to supply whatever you lack? Have you ever stepped out of your personal boat?

If you haven't, I hope you will. And when you do, keep looking (as Peter would no doubt counsel you) at Him.

chapter 8

"Where Are Your Accusers?"

When I first saw her, she looked anything but desirable. Her clothes, what was left of them, were a mess, and scratches and bruises randomly covered her skin. When they dragged her through the inner circle around Jesus at the Temple that morning and flung her to the ground in front of Him, instantly I sensed where they might have found her. I even suspected that they might have set her up. The thoughtful discourse that had just begun changed into an ugly scene. The young woman sprawled awkwardly on the ground in front of us, and the triumphant cadre of scribes and Pharisees surrounding us did not even try to hide their smirks.

"Teacher," the senior Pharisee began with great satisfaction, "this woman has been caught in the very act of adultery!"

A low gasp escaped from the involuntary watchers behind us, and I wondered if their amazement really stemmed from this woman's indiscretion or the brazen audacity of the officials.

"Moses' law requires that we stone women like this! What do you say, sir?"

So that was it. What they really wanted was to make Jesus go on the record and say something that they could later turn against Him. Justice for this poor woman was the last thing on their minds.

I thought the silence would last forever. No one in the crowd was about to leave this gripping scene, no matter how disgusting it was. And Jesus took His time as He considered His response. From His seat in the center of the courtyard He looked at the disgraced figure crouching before Him, her head covering pulled low over her humiliated face. Gently He reached out to push it back. Quickly she turned away. He tried once more, again failing to make eye contact.

As I watched I recognized something in His face that I had seen only a few times before—compassion and sorrow mixed with a rush of anger. I didn't know what was coming, but instinctively I knew He would have the last word about this.

Leaning over, He began writing something with His finger on the paving stones of the Temple portico. From where I was standing what He was writing was upside down, and I didn't want to appear too curious. But the officious Pharisees and their posse could not contain themselves. One by one they began to maneuver themselves into position to see what He was writing.

Even knowing Jesus as well as I did, and even understanding the duplicity of those religious zealots, I could not have predicted what I saw unfolding before my eyes. One after another, as they found a way to peek over Jesus' shoulder, their faces reddened into a full blush, and they turned and fled. Separately. Individually. No consultation with each other. It was as if a big wind had come to blow all the fruit off a tree, but instead of falling to the ground together, every piece flew in a different direction, each on its own tangent.

In very short order we were left with just Jesus, those who had been eagerly listening to Him earlier, and the girl. She still had not moved. This time He spoke directly to her.

"Where are your accusers?" He asked. "Isn't there anyone left to condemn you?"

Timidly she looked around, giving me my first real look at her puffy face. True enough, those cruel men were gone. Of course, she was accustomed to being left behind by men who had no more need of her, but this was different. Her expression turned to one of wonder.

"No one, sir."

"Neither do I condemn you. Go and sin no more." And with those quiet words He extended His hand to help her to her feet, then put His arm around her shoulder and walked away from the group, speaking to her for another few seconds in low tones. I never asked Him—or her—what He said, but the next day she was back. This time she came at her own initiative, not dragged through the street like a criminal. And the next day. And the next.

I don't reveal her name now, because I'm not certain she would want that. But she came to us day after day, immersing herself in the unconditional acceptance that flowed from Jesus, learning something new every day about the true nature of God's kingdom—learning for the first time that not all men were "like that."

She was even there at the end—and beyond. Her awakening began the day the world "used" her for the last time, and in our Master she discovered the true worth of a once-trashed life.

You know them, and so do I. And they are not all girls. Neither are they all in public high school. Teens of both sexes, within the

Adventist school system as well as outside it, are vulnerable to the ebb and flow of peer approval. When it flows, it often sweeps them down emotional riverbeds where danger lies hidden around the next bend, and before they know it they feel as though they've been washed out to sea. And when the approval ebbs, the desperate prospect of losing friends and popularity can drive them to bargains they never expected to be making.

"But she comes from such a wonderful home," we mutter sadly, shaking our wise heads in disbelief about her recent choices. "Her parents must be heartbroken." Trust me, they are. Or worse: "Her parents are going to kill her when they find out!" Sadly, sometimes she thinks they will!

The dollar value, or the cleanliness and respectability of a person's home, are not the determining factors. The intelligence or graduate education of their parents don't add that much either.

Wouldn't it be ironic if we were to discover that the young woman thrust before Jesus at the Temple that morning was the daughter of a Pharisee? It's pretty safe to assume that she wasn't. If that had been the case, the conspirators would have found someone else as their example of debauchery. They would have carefully avoided exposing the failures of one of their own. We still do that today, don't we? Haven't you ever noticed the wilder tendencies of a faculty kid being gingerly overlooked?

Every school has its share of teens who find themselves floating downstream like a piece of driftwood, completely at the mercy of poor choices they have either made or allowed others to make for them—the price, they thought, for keeping friends.

Some are gifted enough to maintain high grades while they're swept from one whirlpool or set of rapids to another, but most struggle academically and soon become completely unmotivated. The parents wring their hands and wail, "Where did we go wrong?" Teachers shake their heads and ask, "What are we going to do with him?"

A thousand different ingredients swirl through the mix in an infinite number of combinations—alcohol, illegal drugs, tobacco, sexual promiscuity, borderline or minor criminal activity (which sometimes escalates beyond a kid's expectations), and fascination/obsession with the popular culture and the latest music and movies.

I know one young man who is so intensely wrapped up in movies that he is virtually unable to carry on a serious conversation about anything else! (I'm not kidding.)

Then we have the teens who are not simply the "dazed and confused" victims of their friends' exploitation. They know what they are doing, and they are precisely where they have chosen to be. One of them boasted to me a while back, "I own my parents! They don't have a clue!"

When we look into the eyes of a kid with that mind-set, what do parents and teachers have to look forward to? I'll tell you. We have the confidence that the Holy Spirit never lets that young person out of His sight for a moment! Resistance, of course, can persist for a long time— long enough to be extremely discouraging to those who pray for them, hurt for them, and make the long drive to pick them up when they're suspended from school or spend the night in a holding cell.

Perhaps resistance persists long enough to saddle parents with the task, unthinkable just months before, of raising a grandchild born out of wedlock.

But at some point all teens find themselves confronted by the Jesus who tenderly reaches out to turn their embarrassed face in His direction and make, so to speak, eye contact. "Why are you here?" He asks quietly. "Why are you in this condition?"

In the midst of that encounter it no longer matters whether the tide of peer influence swept Amanda or Jeremy along, or if she or he is dealing with the consequences of deliberate choices. It doesn't even matter if the arrival was voluntary or, as with the young woman at the Temple, the individual was cast at the feet of Jesus in a craven act of cowardice. The opportunity still comes to hear Him say, "There doesn't seem to be anyone here to condemn you. I don't condemn you either, Jeremy, Amanda. I forgive you. Come, see what it's like to be with Me for a while."

Meanwhile the drama continues daily. The stages are the corridors and restrooms at school, the parking lots, the after-school jobs, the family rooms and bedrooms at home, the computer keyboards late into the night. The actors are the "good kids," the "bad kids" (perceived and identified as such themselves), and the kids who can't quite decide which they are. But in every production the pivotal scene is a dialog with Jesus and a response, for better or worse, to His invitation to be a twenty-first-century disciple.

chapter 9

The Rich Young Ruler

When I caught my first glimpse of him, he was standing at the edge of a noisy group who had brought someone to Jesus for healing. Only he didn't seem to be with them. I remember thinking what a handsome robe he was wearing. It had a wide, deep-red sash bordered with gold. I guessed he was in his late teens or early 20s, although it was hard to tell for sure, because, frankly, I did not have much experience with the upper class.

When the commotion ceased and the people ahead of him had gone their way, he came right up to Jesus and extended his hand. I had to strain to hear him, since he spoke so softly. I didn't know if it was his normal manner, or if he just didn't want to be overheard. At the moment, he had Jesus' attention, and that was all that mattered.

"Good Master, what should I do to inherit eternal life?"

Clearly he had come to the right place. And the initiative he had taken in posing this question to Jesus told us that, on some level, at least, he was a believer. Why ask such a thing unless you expect to receive an authoritative answer?

I wish you could have seen his face when Jesus replied. Such an expressive face. Such eager, flashing eyes.

"You know the commandments," Jesus said. "Do not commit adultery, do not kill, do not steal, do not bear false witness, honor your father and mother."

"Yes, of course!" The young man was beaming broadly now. "I've been doing those things since I was a child!" His manner conveyed perhaps a startled joy that apparently he already had it made. Everything he needed to gain eternal life was in place. He had suspected as much, and now Jesus had confirmed it for him.

But wait. The small physical gap between them closed as Jesus subtly stepped up and reached out, placing His arm around the young man and resting His hand on his left shoulder. His voice lowered a bit as He spoke in quieter, more confidential tones. "There is this one thing," He continued.

The young man's eyes widened a bit as he focused intently on Jesus' soft-spoken words. "Go and sell everything you own. Hand out the profits among the poor people who were just here in front of you a couple of minutes ago. You have so much, and they barely have what they need to survive. When you've done that, you will know where to find Me, and I'd like to have you come and follow Me. Your true treasure will be in heaven."

There was an awkward pause. The young man in the expensive robe and deep-red sash, the young leader with the animated, expressive face, was silent for a moment, staring down at the ground. For a second I thought he started to say something to Jesus, but nothing came out.

Without another word he slowly turned and walked back in the direction from which he had come. Impulsively I said to Jesus, who also had been gazing downward, "I hope You're right. I hope he'll be able to find us in a few days after he distributes all his possessions."

But when He looked at me I read in His eyes that we would never see that young man again. "John," He said with sadness in His voice, "it's easier for a camel to get through the eye of a needle than for a rich man to enter the kingdom of God."

Actually, as events unfolded in those last weeks, I may have seen the young man again. The day after Jesus' arrival in Jerusalem, a Monday morning when there were still a few scattered palm fronds lying in the streets through which He had ridden, I caught a quick glimpse of someone about a block away wearing a beautiful robe as he disappeared inside one of the main trading houses.

Success can be intoxicating. I have known others who enjoyed prosperity or status. Before making important decisions, one always has to be careful to count the cost. The young man in the expensive robe had obviously calculated the price of following Jesus and found it much too great. By sundown he had returned to his life of privilege, sad that eternal life would not be his future, but apparently content that in the world that mattered to him, everything was under control.

In modern times we have come to refer to him as "the rich young ruler." That is, when we mention him at all. Mostly we ignore him, because, really, he isn't one of the major characters of the Bible, or even a major player in Jesus' ministry. He comes onto the stage, virtually without introduction, and, after an extremely brief dialog with Jesus, disappears without a trace. The realization that life after commitment to Jesus would be significantly different from what he had known was enough to kill his interest. An influential person in his own day, he had a chance to loom large in recorded history, but threw it away by being unwilling to leave his comfort zone.

But what might have happened if he had looked a bit further into this new life? What if he had taken the time to interview Matthew or Peter or John? Would discipleship have been any more attractive to him *if he had actually gotten to know a disciple?* Suppose he showed up at your school at 3:00 tomorrow as you are making a break for your car and interviewed *you?* Would his decision be any different?

Don't misunderstand. His choice on the day he came face to face with Jesus Himself reflected his own selfishness. It really isn't likely that more prolonged exposure to the disciples' lifestyle would have caused him to make a different decision. But that was *him.* What about the others? The rich young ruler had the advantage of interacting with Jesus personally. The rich young rulers of the twenty-first century have only the Bible, with which they may or may not be familiar, and the example of twenty-first-century disciples.

I believe that direct encounters with Jesus change lives, and that in our day Jesus uses us as the vehicles for those encounters. And yet I have seen far too many kids experience what should be a life-changing confrontation with Jesus and what He wants from them, only to turn and walk sorrowfully away. Sometimes they say He asks too much. Other times they claim they can't figure out what He's really like, because we who represent Him are phonies.

For some, clearly, the price *is* too high, for in their still-young lives they have simply become too attached to their "stuff." Giving *any of it* up would be unthinkable. "I can't believe that God is that picky," they protest.

But what about the rest? Is it possible that you and I do distort their picture of God by our own choices, our own contradictory and confusing witness? If so, who is responsible for their decision?

You and I may be more like the rich young ruler than we ever suspected.

chapter 10

Mrs. Zebedee

My family had always been a source of comfort and pride. The Zebedee household was a happy one, even with the normal arguments that arise in the best of homes. I don't recall any of us ever having a big fight with each other, or bad feelings that lasted for a long time. When James and I decided to follow Jesus, Mother and Father were surprised, to say the least (we didn't even have a chance to tell Mother goodbye before we left that morning), but in our later contacts with home we could tell they were proud that Jesus had chosen us for this unique ministry.

Father was not especially interested in politics and government. In fact, it was in his best interests to stay out of controversial things, because we had regular customers from a lot of different backgrounds, including Roman officeholders. Also we had to stay in the good graces of the authorities or lose our contract to fish at all. But he did understand the need for our people to be out from under oppressive rule. I think he also recognized that our own Jewish leaders had lost their way. He didn't always agree that faithfulness to God meant what Rabbi Horshon insisted it meant. *But not wishing to stir rebellion in his sons' hearts or to cause trouble in the community, he never spoke much about it.*

James and I were the ones who forced the issue by our sudden radical decision. We would be missed on the family boats, but Father had other employees, and he would be all right. We received nothing but support from home.

Indeed, you could say we had a little too much. As our little band of travelers came and went from Bethsaida, Mother had become acquainted with Jesus. He had been a guest in our home a number of times, eaten at our family table. We sensed what an honor this was, and I noticed that Mother always made sure the neighbors and our extended family knew whenever we hosted Him.

One day, shortly after one of these family dinners, Mother inquired about the personal dynamics of our group.

"So, John," she asked, "which of you does Jesus seem closest to?"

"What do you mean?" I said, responding to her question with a question of my own.

"Surely you've noticed who His favorites are," she said with a sly grin.

Well, truthfully, I hadn't. My family has always said I was oblivious to subtle things like that, and I suppose they're right.

"I don't know," I finally managed. "We all get along very well. He talks to all of us every day, and He gives us assignments suited to our different skills. Maybe He doesn't have a favorite."

"We should do something about that, son," she said in a tone that I recognized as her most purposeful. When Mother started talking like that, she always had something in mind.

The next day before we left to head south again, Mother came into the room that James and I shared and told us her plan. Yes, we knew in advance what she was going to do. And it shames me now that we didn't put a stop to it immediately. But we didn't.

For one thing, we were not accustomed to saying no to Mother. We had been brought up with the understanding that if it was Mother's idea, it was a good one. But I do have to admit that at the time it did actually sound like a good idea. We might have found the courage to talk her out of it if . . . it hadn't sounded so appealing to us.

She waited for just the right moment. It didn't come until we arrived in Jericho en route to Jerusalem. He was walking back to us from the private gardens where we knew He prayed whenever we passed through this area, and she ran to intercept Him.

"Master," she began almost fawningly, "I have a favor to ask."

Jesus received dozens of requests for favors every day, so He was used to it. But I doubt anyone had ever approached Him with this particular request. "What would you like Me to do, Mrs. Zebedee?"

I realize now that He probably knew what was coming. Mother told me later that His eyes seemed to look right into her soul, as if He knew her better than anyone. It was unnerving, and yet she was so intent on her request that she went ahead anyway.

"Master, You know what wonderful young men my sons are. I would hope that You would appoint one to sit at Your right and one at Your left when You come into Your kingdom."

In other words, she felt that we deserved the most important positions of power in God's kingdom. And we did not disagree. What were we thinking? At the distance of several decades I look back and see how stupid we were! How badly we had miscalculated the whole nature of God's order. Jesus had come to show us what God was really like, and we had missed the point so widely that all we could think about was accumulating power in heaven!

I really don't know what we expected Him to say. I've replayed that dialog hundreds of times in my mind. Did we think He was going to light up suddenly and exclaim, "Why, Mrs. Zebedee! Of course! Why didn't I think of that? They would be perfect for the jobs!" (And just exactly what would those jobs involve? We had no idea, of course. None of us had thought that far ahead.)

His actual response, though, was entirely consistent with the Jesus I later came to know much better, and looking back, I can see that there could have been only one outcome to this exchange. Astonishingly, He showed no annoyance. In fact, He was extremely kind, considering the brassy nerve represented by such a selfish petition. His gaze into Mother's soul never wavered, but He did offer a slight smile.

"Mrs. Zebedee, you have no idea what you are asking."

See, Jesus understood that our love for Him was the real thing. He knew us well enough to see that this wild scheme represented only a temptation of the moment, encouraged by our egos and a mother's desire for greatness for her sons. It was not at the core of our relationship with Him. His understanding had penetrated our hearts at the very beginning, and He knew this was not why we were with Him. He also realized that we weren't prepared for what would come.

Turning directly to us, He asked, "Do you think you can drink from the cup that will come to Me? Are you able and willing to endure whatever happens?"

Naively we gave our quick and predictable response. "Yes, Lord, certainly we are able."

"I know you are," He said kindly. "I know. But there is so much that you don't yet understand. And there is much that is in My Father's hands, and not for Me to decide."

We had no idea! *But you know what? We were able. In the end, we were able. Because He was able. And just as it was His sufferings in which we ultimately had to participate, it was His power that enabled us to come through.*

I get letters from the churches and I hear of the struggles over this issue and that, between this believer and that one. And I wish each of them could experience that sweet, direct look from Jesus Himself and hear Him ask, "Is greatness really what you want? Do you realize what you are asking?"

Mother meant well, and He realized that. He might have avoided her afterward, dismissing her as one of those "pushy women." But He didn't. Years later when Mother died, her last thoughts were of the Jesus she had met through James and me, the Jesus who had treated her with such kindness and respect. Her last words to us were not about positioning ourselves at the Master's right and left and making her proud in the kingdom of heaven. Rather, they simply reflected her joy that she would be there. Knowing that she would be there was enough.

The Gospel writers make it clear that John and James were in on this power play. We can't chalk it all up to the overweening pride of Mrs. Zebedee. Nor do we find any indication that they ever tried to prevent her from brokering this attempt at favoritism. To their credit, of course, they later came to appreciate the folly of this approach—indeed, that it was 180 degrees opposed to the ethic Jesus was patiently trying to teach them. Daily He demonstrated the kingdom before their very eyes, but, like us, they were pretty slow to catch on.

Parent-child relationships, profoundly affected as they are by the culture in which they exist, are no doubt very different in the twenty-first century. Not only would our present environment be unrecognizable to the Zebedees, but the expectations that parents and kids have of each other today bear little resemblance to the way family units functioned then.

But human nature is still human nature, and sin is still sin. As a teacher I talk with a lot of parents, and it often amazes me to observe how absolutely convinced many of them are that their kid is "misunderstood," that the system, even in Christian education, fails to accommodate the wonderful unique qualities their child so obviously exhibits. This leads them to run interference for them, plead for opportunities for extra credit, and complain about the unreasonable demands of the school, whether it involves academic standards or the dress code or issues of behavior and discipline. We ask too much, insisting that they be too scholarly, too prompt in turning in assignments, too neatly dressed, too courteous, too honest.

Sooner or later every teacher deals with cheating or some other form of dishonesty. In one year I detected three separate instances of students' downloading research papers (in part or in whole), poems, and other kinds of assignments from the Internet and submitting them as original work for full credit. Reactions vary, of course, but in an alarming number of cases, instead of shame and disgrace at having been discovered, the student and parents both respond with minimal dismay, wishing we wouldn't make such a big deal of it. One of the students who had downloaded a complete research paper told me that *her mother helped her find the Web site and retyped the material, rather than cutting and pasting, so that it would at least look original!*

No wonder family relationships have deteriorated. In many cases it is simply a matter of kids' observing the values and ethics modeled by their parents and losing respect. Paul's cautionary advice to parents to avoid provoking their children to wrath often becomes perverted into a reluctance to set out any expectations for their kids. They must not be asked to be *different*.

The "nurture and admonition of the Lord" (Eph. 6:4) becomes

subject to the prevailing winds of the culture, and educators often discover that they are rowing against tides being pulled by students in the role of the moon, surrounded by a supporting cast of "stars" played by parents, who do little but smile serenely.

But I get to deal with other parents, too. Plenty of them still take the integrity of their kids seriously, doing their best to "train a child in the way he should go" (Prov. 22:6, NIV). It is not a strategy always guaranteed to yield short-term positive results. Some of these faithful parents struggle daily with the disappointment of their children's choices. But they don't throw in the towel, and they don't erect barriers to shield their kids from the consequences of their choices.

Of all the life issues that influence the flavor of every single day of a teenager's life, parent relationships always rank in the top two or three. Each family has to find its own way, because trying to duplicate what worked for the Millers across the street will never, never feel right for everyone else. Besides, the Millers don't have a little brother with a learning disability, or a mom who obsesses over every *last dime*. You get the picture.

How is Jesus calling you to fulfill your discipleship role within your own family? What would He think (actually, that should be what *does* He think) about your relationship with your parents?

Every day I carry close to my heart a teenager who seriously needs professional counseling, but cannot bring himself to tell his parents about his problem. So nothing gets fixed. Next to him in my thoughts is the gifted young woman who has pretty much given up hope that her dad will ever be able to understand that God calls to both of them through spiritual impulses that are equally genuine but very, very different. Unfortunately, his interpretation of this some-what-wider-than-normal generational chasm is that the God she is discovering must be counterfeit. So they rarely discuss it anymore, and when they do, the decibel level rises.

I think of a home with two churchgoing teenagers and two churchgoing parents who, together, equal four extremely unhappy people. What exactly are they unhappy about? No one knows. From time to time one catches a glimpse inside their family circle long enough to realize that each family member is angry not only with the unsympathetic, unforgiving outside world, but also with each other. The siblings form one side, the parents the other. What is really going on here? Again, no one knows, because the circle quickly closes again and the conspiracy of silence resumes. The darkness inside that circle swallows and absorbs all well-meaning inquiries.

Jesus said, "I have come that they may have life, and have it to the full" (John 10:10, NIV). The King James translators chose the word "abundantly." Young disciples of Jesus in the twenty-first century who truly want to go where He leads will understand that the most important mission trip of their lives is their journey home every evening. When they walk through the door to interact with the people who gave them life, the genuineness of their discipleship is on the line. Every succeeding generation has believed that *their* challenges were the toughest. Perhaps your generation is right. And of all your tough challenges, this one may top the list.

If the gospel of Jesus Christ is worth sharing in a small village hospital in Nicaragua or at Ground Zero in Lower Manhattan, it is worth sharing with those who love us the most. Did you know that the Old Testament ends with a prophecy that the last days will see a turning of the generations toward each other, reconciling and repenting? How cool is it to have the opportunity you have every day? You can play a key role in the fulfillment of prophecy in your own home. The Millers across the street can't do it for you.

chapter 11

Zacchaeus

T he day we walked into Jericho that last spring we were with Jesus, a certain uneasiness had begun to spread through our group. Its source was hard to identify. We had been on the road for weeks, first heading north, then circling back around to the south again, gradually working our way toward Jerusalem. In fact, it looked as though we might be in Jerusalem for Passover, and that was an exciting prospect.

In every village we entered it seemed that word had gone ahead to tell that we were coming. We found people of every description waiting at the gate, just to get a glimpse of Jesus. The crowds were sometimes fairly demanding, as if getting a few minutes in Jesus' presence were something to which they were entitled. It could be most annoying, and yet for some reason the inner perimeter right around Jesus was almost always an oasis of calm, even serenity.

Those of us in the traveling party were often separated from each other and left to fend for ourselves. But if we could snag a few minutes right in the epicenter of the action to watch Jesus at close range as He *spoke quietly with those who were in pain, or who had some theological question that had been troubling them, it was possible to forget briefly the hundreds of people impatiently waiting their turn.*

The only clue we had that Jesus tired of this was the fatigue we saw on His face and heard in His voice in the evenings when we sat by our campfire. When He reached out His hand to stop a fever in its tracks, or listened to a little girl ask Him what God is like, you would never have known the toll it was taking on Him. In fact, we thought He was at His best when He was surrounded by kids. Intuitively they trusted Him. Dozens of children were always darting in and out of the scene.

"Watch me, Jesus!" would suddenly ring out, and an 8-year-old would come careening through the irritated adults, doing a somersault ending in a handstand. Jesus always noticed. And He always said something to that particular child that they would remember their whole lifetime.

After a grueling day Jesus' idea of relaxing often involved just sitting on the ground with His back against a tree, telling stories to the children of whatever town we were in at the time. For many of them He was the very first person outside their own families who regarded them as significant in any way. He was almost a magnet for the needy—not just the poverty-stricken, a category that included most people in these towns, but the emotionally needy, people who desperately longed to feel special but never did.

As we arrived in Jericho on this particular spring day, the usual turmoil slowed our progress into town as the hundreds of gloriously happy mingled with the merely curious. We had almost arrived at the large market square when Jesus came to an abrupt stop and looked up and to His left. I followed His gaze, as did the eyes of dozens packed in closely around Him.

In the branches of a sycamore, just beginning to leaf out as the days grew longer and warmer, we saw a man—a very small man.

"Zacchaeus, you no-good . . . ," someone right beside me yelled very loudly and not very nicely, using language that I won't repeat. You get the picture. "What are you doing up there? Get down from Mrs. Zurfink's tree and get out of here! You're going to snap off that limb! Can't you see you're distracting the Master? You're an embarrassment!"

"Oh, give him a break," sneered a voice on the other side of me. "He's such a tiny 'bite' of manhood, the tree hasn't even noticed he's there!" The crowd erupted in laughter. Well, it was pretty funny.

By now the little man's face was growing red, and he turned his back on the crowd to scramble down from his perch.

At that moment I heard a familiar voice—and it wasn't laughing. "Yes, Zacchaeus. Do come down. I'd like to meet you. In fact, I think we'll come to your house for lunch."

A reaction of general disbelief, then embarrassment, swept through the crowd. It was an awkward moment as the stunned little man did indeed return to street level and slowly made his way into Jesus' inner circle, which rapidly—and quietly—cleared a path for him.

On the way to Zacchaeus's house I learned a little about him from those who still hung around the edges of our group. When I heard he was a tax collector, I understood immediately. People naturally regarded him as corrupt, and it was probably true. In addition, he bore the signs of a really obnoxious personality. Fortunately, the presence of Jesus had a subduing effect on that, but one could still see a pretty rough, crude character in Zacchaeus.

As much as I learned about Zacchaeus that day in Jericho, I discovered even more about Jesus' care and concern for even the undesirables of society. I had always observed that He treated them kindly, that He spoke as gently with them as with anyone else. But on this day Jesus invited Himself and all His friends into the home of some-one whom we would never have chosen to visit on our own. It took His love to propel us into Zacchaeus's neighborhood, down his crooked lit-tle street, and across the threshold into that infamous house, furnished with lovely things acquired fraudulently.

During our entire stay at Zacchaeus's place many from the crowd that had been surrounding us milled about in the street in stunned be-wilderment. Occasionally we would hear someone shout out, but mostly it was just a dull group grumble. From my place at the table I couldn't hear much of the conversation between Jesus and His aston-ished host, but I remember the amazement of everyone, including Zacchaeus's family, when the little man suddenly stood.

"Friends," he began somewhat nervously, "I have been troubled for many years, and it has not been easy for my family to live with the resentment and anger that flows toward us daily from all over Jericho. But today my conscience will no longer churn inside me. Look around you at my beautiful home. What you see will soon be sold, and half the profits will be donated to those in need. Furthermore, if anyone be-lieves I have assessed their tax obligation unfairly, I will restore to them four times as much as they deserve!"

Now it was the guests' turn to be astonished. No one had seen this coming. We looked at each other as if to ask, "What could Jesus have said to him to cause this?"

The silence was short-lived. Almost at once we heard Jesus' quiet voice calmly say, "Today salvation has come to this house. The Son of man has come to seek and to save those who are lost."

As we withdrew to leave Jesus alone with the family for a moment that none of them but Jesus had dreamed of, there were tears and em-braces, and then the head of the household strode confidently out into the street to make the same announcement to the public he had wronged for so many years. When we left Jericho that day it was, in many respects, a different community. Salvation had indeed come to Zacchaeus's home, scores of festering wrongs all over town were being set right, and Jesus' ministry had again had a transforming effect upon human misery.

Night was coming on—in more ways than one. We had spent the prime hours of afternoon there, and literal darkness would soon fall. But we were also entering the closing days of Jesus' time with us. If only we had known. So much closer to Him we would have walked. So much more eagerly we would have listened. So many more questions we would have asked. So much more love we would have shown.

I've thought many times of that day in Jericho. What was it that opened the way for a crook like Zacchaeus to be restored to honor . . . instantly? Why was complete forgiveness . . . immediate? I've concluded that it was just because he asked. And that's why we were in Jericho that day in the first place. There was a little man—again, in more ways than one—in that town who was hated by everyone, including himself. Jesus arrived just at lunchtime to seek and to save that one hated little man, as well as all those who would see this act and begin to grasp the reality of the kingdom of heaven.

Zacchaeus's self-esteem problem isn't all that difficult to understand. No one liked him. In fact, since very few people in Jericho even wanted to be seen with him, it's interesting to speculate about how much—or how little—experience his wife might have had entertaining dinner guests. Maybe *she* is the unseen hero in this story, having thrown together a meal for Jesus and His disciples on such short notice.

Most teens don't live daily under the kind of cloud that hovered over Zacchaeus's house. But we know that an alarming number of high school students trudge gamely from one class to another, day after day, feeling inadequate, physically unattractive, dumb, and generally unpopular. Some show it; others don't. A number have brought it on themselves by their antisocial behavior. Others are simply not blessed with natural people skills or social grace and just don't know where to begin to transform themselves into one of the "cool" kids.

"I'm just a boring person," a freshman girl said to me a few years ago. Her comment startled me, because I did not find her boring at all. But she was convinced that she was. In her case, it seemed to be a self-fulfilling prophecy, though, because sure enough, she really had very few friends. I had always assumed she preferred it that way.

I think of one young man who truly seemed to have *no* close friends, but to whom it didn't seem to matter that much. He cared not a whit for the feelings of others and would blurt out some fairly outrageous comments, letting the chips fall wherever the chips fell. When the bell rang at the end of class, you hoped you weren't between him and the door, because *nothing and no one* was allowed to deter him from his rapid progress to the next class. He was there to *learn* and to make good grades, and, literally, nothing else mattered. If something appeared in one of his textbooks, or a remark was made in class, that he deemed silly or especially unenlightened, he swiftly delivered his judgment.

I often wondered if it was his behavior that caused him to have no friends, or if it was really the other way around—he behaved this way as a defense mechanism to reassure himself of his importance, because no one else saw him as worth their time.

We don't know if Zacchaeus's social isolation was a condition that came naturally to him, or whether he just made a series of life choices that eventually ostracized him and identified him as the loner he had become. Whatever the cause, the little man who climbed that sycamore tree in Jericho felt he had reason to regard himself rather poorly.

But when low self-esteem comes face to face with Jesus, it has no chance. When Jesus passed beneath his perch and Zacchaeus suddenly found himself involuntarily hosting Him for lunch, what could he have said?

"Uh, well, I appreciate that, Master, but if You could see my house You'd understand; You really don't want to go there. And I'm pretty boring, myself. What would we talk about? My wife is a lousy cook. Trust me, it's not a good idea."

I don't think so. Jesus reached down into that stale and parched personality, stiffened by crooked business dealings, and brought to the surface a sparkling, joyful, generous disciple who vowed he would stop at nothing until his behavior persuaded everyone in town that he wasn't who they thought he was.

Jesus could have surveyed the damage done by this small-bodied, small-minded man, denounced him, and miraculously restored every farthing he had swindled from the people of Jericho. He could have gone to every house in town, dragging Zacchaeus along, saying, "Sir, I hereby restore to you fourfold what this shameful public servant has stolen from you," then produced the cash on the spot.

Instead, He changed Zacchaeus. Through the power of Jesus, it was the tax collector himself who *wanted* to make things right. He had longed to be a good person all along. Jesus alone enabled him to believe in himself.

I know teens who are starving for belief in themselves. And I know where they can find it. Why don't we tell them?

chapter 12

"Have Pity on Us"

Companionship with Jesus took new forms of adventure almost every day. Our lives were not easy. Always we had new obstacles to overcome or new ideas to discuss as we walked along or paused in some meadow for lunch. He was continually giving us new truths about the kingdom of God that we had never considered before, and often He would work around to things by asking us questions.

"What do you hear the people saying about Me?" He asked us one evening. "Who do they think I am?" We had a variety of answers to this, of course, but He immediately made the question more personal: "Who do you say that I am?"

It was just like Jesus to be direct. He beat around the bush only if it was absolutely necessary to bring someone along gently or slowly, helping that person to discover truth at just the right moment. Most of the time He confronted our thinking head-on.

"Whom do you say that I am?" drew a challenge that we could no longer avoid. Not that we wanted to—we were committed to our Master as the Messiah sent from God. But He knew that we needed *to hear ourselves say it. Commitment is more real when you can actually express it. So is desire.*

One day near Jericho—a typical day, actually—our noisy, chaotic entourage slowly moved down the road, when off to the side I caught a glimpse of two blind men sitting just far enough onto the road's shoulder so as not to get trampled. A good idea it was, too, because few in the mob around us were paying any attention to where they were going. Once people got this close to Jesus they became entirely focused on getting His attention, persuading Him of their need, or sometimes impressing Him with their lack of it—either showing off their knowledge of the law or reciting their good deeds. You know the type. Tiresome? Yes. But every crowd has a few of them. Now, decades later, I can see that human nature is still the same. But I digress.

I may have been the only one who noticed the blind men until suddenly one of them yelled, "Lord, have pity on us, You Son of David!"

Instantly Jesus froze. Searching out the source of the plea, His eyes bore in on the two pathetic figures sitting cross-legged in the trash and other debris that always accumulates beside a busy road. They had called Him "Son of David," signifying their belief in Him as the promised Messiah. In response to that kind of unquestioning belief dwelling deep in the hearts of these poverty-stricken men who couldn't even see Him, Jesus would at that moment have done almost anything they wanted.

So once again I would learn something new about my Lord. It was obvious what they needed, so I expected He would just take a moment to stoop down and touch their eyes. After He restored their vision we would continue on. Remarkable? Of course, but we were becoming quite accustomed to little scenes like this playing out in front of us, and we had started to anticipate Jesus' reaction to people.

But that's not exactly what happened. Without even a moment of reflection Jesus confronted both men with the question of a lifetime. "What do you want Me to do for you?" He asked.

Until then there had been nothing to indicate that this would be a special moment. But it has become one of the memories I cherish the most. The men did not hesitate.

"Lord, what we want is that our eyes should be opened!" They wanted to see—to share the experience that everyone else around them seemed to have. What was so great about eyesight? They didn't know. In fact, they really had no idea how profoundly their lives were about to change. But they had heard about sight and vision since they were little boys, and now they believed Jesus could give them what they wanted.

In an instant it was done. The Master of the universe reached out and touched the eyes of both men—and the first thing they saw was His face. As I sit on this island looking out to sea I review the scenes of my life that I spent at Jesus' side. The look of astonishment on those men's faces is one that I think of quite often. Neither of them knew what to expect, really, but if it was to come from the hand of Jesus, they were ready for anything.

I saw those men often after that. Unlike so many whom Jesus healed, they did not forget or forsake Him. They traveled along with us, and as long as I knew them, they never tired of looking again at that face that was their first image. But they didn't stop with that. I began to observe that as we entered a new region, they would often run ahead of us and seek out people for Jesus to help. Again and again I would hear one of them say to a skeptical recruit, "All you have to do is ask Him. He did what I asked of Him, and He will do it for you."

The totality of what the Lord did for these men went far beyond their regaining their sight. He had restored to them a purpose as well.

They not only had eyesight; they had a life. All because when Jesus asked them what they wanted Him to do, they told Him.

Several times as I prepared this chapter I paused to wonder how well equipped teens today are to answer "the question." How would you react if Jesus unexpectedly strolled down the hallway of your high school, spotted you, smiled, and asked, "Stephanie, Justin, what do you want Me to do for you?"

When I actually framed this scenario for my English class, I came away with a bunch of pretty bland answers—proof that at least that group of teens (don't get me wrong—I love them!) hadn't given it much thought.

I suppose the response that brought me up short was this one: "I would ask Him for assurance that I am going to heaven, because I don't always feel that I should, or even that He wants me to."

Wow. Are we, your teachers, doing this poor a job when we discuss our assurance of salvation? Not too long ago I took a young man out to dinner, hoping to get to know him a little better. I was aware that he had been involved in some pretty risky behavior, but there were other people to whom he was being held accountable for that. My purpose was simply to let him know that I still believed in him and to see how I could help him believe in himself.

Over dinner we talked about a lot of things, until finally I was able to ask him to describe his level of spiritual interest. To my delight, I discovered that notwithstanding some evidence to the contrary, he really did have an interest, but he turned right around and discouraged me by what he said next: "I know," he finished, "that before I can have a relationship with God I'm going to have to change some things in my life." Oh.

And so we have yet another case of the patient's attempting to perform surgery on themselves before consulting the doctor. I know his perspective is not restricted to him alone. It's not even limited to teens. I believe a lot of young people pick it up from observing adults trying to fix themselves before seeking a relationship with Jesus. They see it from breakfast till bedtime. And too often they observe it in the fronts of their classrooms.

Why do we so easily forget that Jesus took people exactly the way He found them? He didn't expect them to change themselves and then follow Him. He changed them Himself—He brought the healing.

Once they had looked into that face, though—once they had experienced that touch—no one wanted to go back to their blindness or leprosy. And once we too have looked into that face and experienced that touch, we don't want to return to the keg party or the sexual sin.

I am also amazed when I encounter teens who have accepted Christ and given themselves to Him, but who somehow cannot seem to find their spot in the parking lot labeled "saved."

Maybe we confuse them by disagreeing with the "once saved, always saved" belief, which teaches that having once given their heart to God, people can never turn their back on that relationship and be lost. You probably know enough about Scripture to understand that such a belief isn't biblical—God never removes from us our freedom to make a different choice, even when He's ahead in the score and we're on His side. We can be lost after having been saved.

But . . . how and why does this translate into uncertainty? Check out John 6:47. What is Jesus really saying here? It's as if He were looking right at the twenty-first-century reader of John's Gospel and saying, "If you have chosen Me—if you genuinely believe in Me—it is settled."

Yes, we will spend every day of our earthly lives growing in our understanding of God, learning how to better reflect His character to the people He places in our paths. But do we think God really wants us to pass those same days "hoping" we will make it to

93

heaven? That must cause God to become very sad. And I suspect it makes Him angry that we who claim to understand how salvation by grace really works would allow today's teens to fall into that mentality. Any student who leaves an Adventist academy convinced that there might just be some hope for them to be saved if only they can somehow manage to get straightened around and not keep screwing up is a student who has been shown a distorted picture of God. The Christian authority figures in their lives will have to answer for it.

But back to the original question: If Jesus came down your high school corridor tomorrow morning, walked over to you and placed His hand on your shoulder, and asked, "Michelle, what do you want Me to do for you?" or "Mike, what do you need from Me right now?" what would you say? If you haven't ever given it much thought, maybe you should. He stands there every day at your very side, waiting for you to respond.

chapter 13

The Widow

We never would have noticed her. I imagine she was one of those people who live in the shadows of every town. Short, beginning to age, stooped over a bit, perhaps not from any crippling illness, but just from the cumulative effects of a life of hard work and not much reward—this woman came and went about her life pretty much unobserved.

She could not have known that today she would be noticed. And amazingly, when she left she still did not know that anyone had seen her.

The woman appeared on this busy afternoon at one of the Temple collection boxes we call "the trumpets," because that's how they are shaped. Passing by the box nearest her, she opened her gnarled fingers and dropped two lepta through the opening. It's the thinnest coin in our currency, worth only a fraction of a cent! Most people won't even stop to pick them up off the street.

Then she was gone. And that would have been the end of it were it not for the eyes of Jesus. He had purposely taken a place near the box to watch people as they brought their offerings. I had never observed

Him do this before, but then Jesus often did new things, so I didn't think it that unusual at the time.

"Did you see that?" He turned to Andrew and me. "Did you see what she did?"

Well, yes, actually, both of us had "seen," but to be truthful, both the woman and the event were so unremarkable that we had not really been paying attention. We wondered what He was getting at.

"It was only two mites," Jesus continued. "That woman's offering was just a couple of simple lepta. If those coins roll off the table when the priests dump the money out of the box, they won't even care. They won't realize those are the most important pieces of money they have."

What? Andrew and I glanced at each other and chuckled. "Why would her lepta be the most important money?" Andrew asked.

"It was all she had," Jesus said so quietly that we had to strain to hear Him. "It was all she had."

In the next few moments we sat fascinated while He told us some things about this woman whom He had never met. She was a widow. Her husband had died quite suddenly perhaps a decade ago, and her life now consisted of sweeping out other people's homes and gleaning in the fields after harvest. In reality she had virtually nothing and no one.

"We have sat here," Jesus told us, "and watched people parade through the Temple toward these boxes, often timing their arrival so that certain others would see them, then producing with a flourish a brightly colored purse containing several polished coins, which they proceed to drop into the box with the loudest clang possible. They aren't subtle about it. In fact, they see nothing wrong with it. And afterward they won't even miss the money. Perhaps they might not even remember how much they gave.

"But this woman came into My house hoping that no one would

notice that she had so little to give. And no one did, except Me. She could have kept one of the lepta to buy a little something to eat on the way home. Instead she gave everything. I will remember."

That was many years ago. Somewhere in the hills outside Jerusalem I know there is a grave, most likely unmarked, where the body of an elderly woman rests. I can imagine that she spent her last hours without fear, because the little woman I saw in the Temple that day had a faith strong enough to see her through to the hour of death. As far as I know, she died completely unaware that her sacrifice had mattered to anyone but her. What a surprise she has waiting!

Teachers and parents expend a huge amount of energy trying to teach teens to use their heads. Been there. Done that. Am there. Do that. Then after all our lectures and eye rolls and exasperated tones of voice, we run into a story like this. I'm sorry, but the little woman in the Temple just didn't use her head. She took the last money she had and, probably without knowing where any more would come from (or when), she threw every bit of it into the collection box and walked away. Reckless.

Do you really suppose she believed that God needed her money? Is it even possible that she could fail to notice all the pushy, showy, obnoxious people noisily "sacrificing" amounts that might have supported her frugal needs for the rest of her life? Think about it. When the well-dressed middle-aged man sitting next to you in church whips out his pen during the offering appeal and proceeds to write a check with several zeroes at the end, how motivated are you to dig around in your pocket and pull out next week's gas money? Don't you need that $5 bill more than God does?

Yep. Clearly you do. Quickly—stuff that $5 back into your

pocket! Whew. You were almost an idiot! An idiot who would have been walking everywhere by next Tuesday afternoon instead of driving.

Here comes the offering plate. The man licks the flap of his tithe envelope in a self-satisfied manner. He has carelessly(?) left his checkbook lying open on the pew next to you, and you sneak a peek at his running balance. Oh, wow. Apparently not all the zeroes went onto the check. Once that baby clears on Monday, he will still have plenty left!

Just let the plate pass. Obviously, once the deacons have finished with the collection there will be more than enough for the church electric bill/Costa Rica mission trip/worthy student fund (aren't you a worthy student?)/summer camp improvement/prison ministry songbooks, or whatever. Gas in the tank is a good thing.

There the plate goes.

Wait! As if in a slow-motion movie scene, you see yourself impulsively stretch across the friend on your other side and retrieve the plate, to the irritation of the deacon who was just reaching for it. You're frantically digging for the $5. Out comes a piece of paper. No! It's the note from Katelyn! Back into the pocket. There it is!

OK, by the time the deacon finally gets the plate, you've unintentionally made as big a show as the gazillionaire with his check. But what have you really done?

The offering plate has $5 more than it had just a moment before. But that's not it. You are represented in that offering plate. No, you are now riding down the aisle in that plate. You have been reckless—you have given God a piece of yourself that you're not quite sure how you are going to replace.

I think Jesus still sits and watches for people, including teens, who are willing to cast caution aside and follow their hearts by committing everything to Him. Does this mean physically emptying our pockets or wallets at church every week? Maybe, maybe not. I believe it involves a much broader approach than that. I think it calls for us to stay alert 24/7 for moments when God invites us to do something really daring—occasions when something radical must be attempted for the kingdom, and we are the ones who are privileged to be in that spot at that moment . . . and willing.

Yeah, we still want you to use your head. We'll still keep reminding you. But you know what? You make us the most proud when you follow your heart. God doesn't want your $5 bill nearly as much as He does you. And although He is willing to wait until the offering appeal next Sabbath (or even some Sabbath in the distant future), He would rather have you now.

chapter 14

The Ten Bridesmaids

W*e never tired of Jesus' stories. Telling a story well is an art, of course, and He was a master of it. Now, it wasn't just that His stories were interesting, but that inevitably they led to a lesson or truth we had never seen before. Every story pointed toward the kingdom. Every one featured a fresh approach to the kingdom. And every one ended with one of us, or someone else in His circle of listeners, gasping, "Oh! Now I get it."*

But of course, not everyone grasped His point. Just as often, others would walk away shaking their heads and wondering what they had missed. Some would never "get it."

It was that way with the parable of the 10 virgins, or bridesmaids. Many of us who heard Jesus tell the parable had actually seen similar scenarios play themselves out in real life. The whole wedding culture of our time featured elaborate celebrations that went on for days at a time, with lots of anticipation and preparation, even an element of mystery. Each step in the celebration was dramatic and filled with symbolism and meaning. And one never knew for sure when the bridegroom would appear. It was bad taste to hurry such things along. The bridegroom showed up when he decided to, and not a moment before. Watching for him could sometimes be an endurance game.

So when Jesus told His parable, it had a familiar ring. Everyone present either had had or knew someone who had had the experience of storing up lamp oil in preparation for the groom's arrival. Some had even had the bad luck to forget this crucial detail until it was too late and the market had closed for the night. But it was left to Jesus to lay this common experience out as a metaphor for the kingdom. Afterward, I would say to myself, "Of course! Why didn't I think of that?"

I suppose what I find most disturbing so many years later is that even understanding the story's symbolism—even recognizing clearly the dangers of growing weary and failing to prepare for my Lord's return— I find it is still very easy to let the oil run low. I get busy. I do really important things. And I forget to watch for Him. I know He's coming. I tell people He's returning. I prepare them. But as the days and months pass with the fulfillment of the promise still in the future, it is so easy to get distracted. So easy to run out of oil.

William Barclay, one of my favorite authors, wrote, "The most dangerous day in a man's life is when he learns that there is such a word as tomorrow." How did Barclay know me? Or my students?

I impose a point penalty for work submitted late in my English classes. Some of my colleagues will not accept tardy work at all. But understanding my own tendency to do things at the last possible moment (or beyond), I have never had the heart to be that severe. Maybe I am letting my students down by not holding them to a stricter standard. One of my former students in particular will recognize himself on this page. He graduated from academy several years ago now, but whenever I see him I ask him if he has finished his research paper yet. He works these days on Capitol Hill for a member of Congress, so I truly hope he has learned to come to terms with deadlines. I went through agonies with this guy (so did other teachers, I might add), who in all other respects was and is a wonderful person and a dear friend with immense leadership potential.

How late is too late? Life throws deadlines at all of us, and over the course of our experience we usually learn which ones have a little flexibility built into them and which refuse to yield by even an hour. Perhaps it really isn't good for us to know such things.

But how do we watch for Jesus? Should we run outdoors a couple times a day to scan the eastern sky for His cloud? I don't know anyone who does that. Should we place dramatic interpretations on news events that seem to fit in with prophecies about His return? Unfortunately, I do know people who do exactly that.

Of course, anyone who understands Scripture and takes the warnings of Jesus seriously can "see the day approaching" (Heb. 10:25). But we have observed it approaching for a long time now, at least from our own warped perspective. As a child, I was afraid that Jesus would come before I had a chance to grow up—or more specifically, before I had a chance to get my driver's license. Well, that day certainly came and went. (I believe the year was 1964.) I made it. Now my daughters have their driver's licenses. It won't be all that long until my son has one. Still, Jesus has not returned.

I suspect that every generation of young Adventists has included plenty who want to spend eternity with Jesus, but are secretly hoping that it doesn't happen too soon. They want to graduate, have a career, and get married. Some will even be honest enough to tell you they want time to get "stuff." Then Jesus can come.

In case we are judging too harshly, let us include those who would be perfectly willing to set aside those earthly goals and go with Jesus whenever He chooses to return, but . . . they are really

103

kind of busy right now, you know, and, oops! "Uh, do you have any oil? Looks like I'm out."

Lost in the mists of the 1950s and 1960s, long ago having given way to this generation's repertoire of praise choruses, is an old gospel song, "We Know Not the Hour." Your parents may remember it:

> "He will come,
> Let us watch and be ready;
> He will come."

When I was a volunteer firefighter in academy, our chief taught us to keep a pair of pants, belt threaded through the loops, lying on the floor within easy reach of our bed. Beneath the pants were our shoes. If the siren blew during the middle of the night, I could have my pants and shoes on and be headed for my dorm room door in about three seconds. All of us could, in turn, run to the firehouse, be on the pumper truck (it was a 1946 Chevy—don't laugh!) and be off campus on our way to the fire in three minutes. The trick, of course, was—you guessed it—hearing the siren in the first place. Sometimes, regretfully, the only action we would see on a given night would be after someone dragged us out of bed to help clean up the returned trucks and their equipment. If you slept through the alarm, everyone on campus knew about it by breakfast.

We have all been "foolish virgins" in one respect or another. Some of us sleep on. Jesus asked us to watch.

So what if it happens before you've had a chance to start your own company or experienced sex or been to Europe? Do you really imagine, even if you haven't yet reached those milestones in this life, that finding yourself in heaven face to face with Jesus could possibly be a disappointment?

At the end of the story, of course, the bridegroom did come. He arrived much later than many had expected. But he still came. I don't like to think much about the ones who were still out looking for places to buy oil. I just remember that those who had prepared were delighted to see him, and they went into the feast with him.

And there was great joy.

chapter 15

Tale of
the Talents

T he last week before Passover was such a swirling vortex of events that even now it can be difficult for me to sort out all the images in my memory. Jesus managed to do quite a lot of teaching that week, and His parable of the talents was one of the most memorable and poignant. It didn't really sink in at the time, but later I realized He was simply laying out the basic plan for our lives after He had gone.

He told of the wealthy man preparing to leave on a long journey who called together his servants and apportioned his assets to them to manage during his absence. To one he gave five talents, to another two, and to the remaining employee he entrusted just one talent. (Talents, by the way, are, you will remember, a certain weight or unit of silver or gold. A talent was a lot of money.)

Jesus didn't take the time to explain why the man in his story drew such distinctions among his employees, probably because it really didn't matter why. The assets were, after all, his to dispose of as he chose. It wasn't a question of equity so much as one of responsibility. Perhaps *he gave each servant the degree of responsibility he knew each could manage well. Then he was off.*

The servant who received five talents of gold or silver to manage invested it in a way that would yield a high return, and sure enough, by the time his boss returned home he had 10 talents to show for his efforts. While the boss was impressed, probably he was not surprised. Perhaps he had chosen this employee for this honor in the first place because he had a great deal of confidence in him. But we don't know that.

Interestingly, though he had been given fewer talents in the first place, the second servant also managed to take his two talents and produce a 100 percent increase on the investment. Upon the boss's return, he came forward with a total of four. Again, the wealthy man was pleased and said so.

But the story takes a downward turn when the boss approaches the third servant. I can actually picture the servant reluctantly shuffling forward to meet the man, head down, hands behind his back.

"Well, sir . . . you know, I'm really just a little afraid of you, sir. I mean, you are known as a hard man. You drive a shrewd business deal and are way out of my league. And, uh, I was, uh, afraid I might lose what you gave me, and I certainly didn't want to take a chance on that! So here, sir, is the talent you gave me. I have kept it safe in that field over there." With that he dusts off some of the dirt from the coins or ingots and hands them back to their rightful owner.

The disgust is plain on the boss's face. He had not asked all that much. But all he had to show for his investment was what he had to start with. What a waste!

"You could at least have put the talent with the bankers to lend for interest," he said. "Did you not even let my own money work for me?"

Quickly he grabbed the talent back from the hapless servant and turned it over to the one who had turned five talents into 10. Now the man had 11.

The boss had not expected miracles. He had given each servant all that they needed to be successful, each at their own rate. It was the servant who failed even to try that brought the disappointment.

"The kingdom of heaven is like this," Jesus said. Only a few days later He was gone, leaving behind a clear lesson in what He expected of us. To each of us He had given different gifts. From each of us He expected different results. But He knew that we would know what to do with those gifts.

In the decades since I heard Jesus tell that story I have watched my fellow disciples develop so many thrilling gifts on behalf of His kingdom. It is almost as if many of them retell Jesus' parable to themselves from time to time, reminding themselves that He gave us everything we need to do what He wants us to do.

I have also seen a fair number of talents buried in the field, so to speak. Often when the servant goes back to use the one talent they have received, they cannot even find it.

Many of those who started out with me in the early days right after Jesus left us took their gifts and grew so dramatically that sometimes we could scarcely recognize them. They accomplished far more than they had ever dreamed they could. All because they took the Master at His word.

If you knew Brian the way I do, I think you would like him. Don't get me wrong—not everyone appreciates him, but he's a pretty neat guy. He is an excellent cellist and takes his talent seriously. Could he be a professional cellist? I don't know, but at this point he is interested in being the best cellist he can be. He also writes passably good political satire. It makes me laugh, anyway, and I'm on the opposite side of almost every issue from Brian!

Peter is a gymnast, graceful, fun to watch. He can not only do all those daring routines, he coaches young children and teaches them the moves he has mastered. But that isn't Peter's only talent. He's also a very good sketch artist. And you should see the walking sticks he whittles!

When I survey the astonishing talents of the young people I have known in recent years, I close my eyes and hear Lori finishing a Sarasate piece on her violin and getting a standing ovation from a packed house; I see Denise's portrait photography that can magnify her subject's personality, and Rob's gift of being able to write a column and nearly always make me laugh out loud; I remember proofreading papers by Justin that hardly needed any editing at all; I am overwhelmed by the brilliance of Ryan's intellect; I admire the leadership skills and idealism of Kyle; then I come to JJ, probably the true twenty-first-century Renaissance person.

The most important quality these kids share is the understanding that God expects them to develop their talents and use them to help and encourage others. Most of them have multiple skills and abilities. All of them take care to preserve and enlarge their gifts.

Then there are the students who contribute to us in ways we often do not categorize as talents. At my school Heather has apparently decided that holding the door open for people should be her ministry. Between class periods we see her holding the heavy glass doors open for dozens of students streaming in and out of our buildings. (I happen to know that Heather has other skills. I hear she is an excellent horsewoman and rides in equestrian competitions.) Then I remember Gabe's thoughtful compassion for a grieving faculty member. I am impressed by the willingness of Shawn, now an alumnus, to come back to his alma mater and work with the chaplain's office to give Bible studies and mentor younger students.

All of them seem to catch the point of the parable of the talents. They have grasped the principle of accountability. God holds them responsible for their gifts. Have you inventoried your gifts? How many can you identify?

Remembering Jesus' story, which character received the condemnation from the master? The one who had received only one talent, of course. Did the master criticize him because he had fewer talents than the others? No, that had nothing to do with it. The master's harsh words came in response to the servant's indifference. He thought it didn't matter—he would just bury his single talent and keep it safe. When the master returned, all could see that nothing had changed. It was in exactly the same condition in which he had received it. The servant had accomplished nothing great with it, because he had attempted nothing great.

All around us today are young twenty-first-century followers of Jesus acting on the conviction that He calls them to aspire to something much bigger than they are. Even Jesus Himself grew "in wisdom and stature, and in favour with God and man" (Luke 2:52).

The master in the parable returned to find mixed results. But our Master has not yet returned. If you have left your talent buried in the field, there still may be time—today—to find and retrieve it. What are you waiting for?

chapter 16

"Feed My Lambs"

I n the closing years of my life not a single day passes that I don't in memory revisit that hill on that Friday. I never watch thunderclouds form over the Mediterranean without recalling the brilliant lightning that ripped through our souls the day that noon was dark as midnight.

That day has no rival for the most horrendous of my life. Laying my own family members in their graves did not compare to the devastation I endured as I looked up at that crude wooden cross and saw the Lord of my life giving His.

Indeed, the only reason I can bring myself to tell it now is that I must. Without the horror of that experience I would be drowning in my own sins. And so would you.

The years we had spent at His side had brought healing to literally thousands, had brought breath back to some whose breath was gone, and, one by one, had revealed to us the truths about God that the evil one had been so effective in blurring. We believed that Jesus was the promised Messiah even though we still had not grasped its full meaning. Our picture of God's triumph over evil was so incomplete! And so simplistic.

The foreshadowing that Jesus offered us again and again, even on that last Thursday night at supper, seems so obvious in retrospect. But we didn't get it. Not until later that night in the garden when events started spinning out of control did we ever seriously consider that the establishment of the kingdom of heaven had a downside.

The element of fear had never been characteristic of my life. But that night I was afraid. We were all afraid. Was our belief in Jesus genuine? Yes. Never doubt it. But was it strong enough to see us through the events rushing upon us?

Nights can seem long when you are troubled and sleep refuses to come. But that night as we hovered like cowards in the shadows, monitoring every transfer of Jesus from one court or palace to another, feeling abjectly helpless, occasionally fearing for our own lives, daylight seemed only a distant memory. There is no way to reproduce the feeling. Nor would you want me to.

I was standing close enough to hear Peter, who had become one of my dearest friends, loudly and profanely swear that he had nothing to do with this Jesus. You wouldn't want me to reproduce that feeling either. Imagine the overheard betrayal of your closest friend and multiply it a thousandfold; then maybe you can begin to understand.

I need not recount every detail, relive every hour. You know the story. But I saw it happen. I was there to witness Him emerge from the judgment hall under the weight of that abominable cross, and I knew what it meant. Only His Father could save Him now. I even tried to think of ways that that might happen. Maybe some of these very Roman soldiers were really angels!

"That's it!" *I convinced myself.* "That's how it will happen!"

Then as the sky darkened and thunder rampaged across that incredible scene I remembered the Jesus who had demonstrated His mastery of the natural elements. If He could quiet a storm, perhaps He had started this one, and it would be His cover for escape.

None of those things happened. Instead the bleeding, dying Jesus whom I loved so much looked directly down at me and said, "Son, behold your mother." I knew immediately what He meant. Mary was right next to me. A beautiful woman of beautiful character, she was in her late 40s. After all that she had done for Him, He wanted to make certain that her needs were provided. She deserved nothing less. In my case, being a disciple of Jesus would mean carrying out the obligation He felt to the unique woman who, having received her life from Him, had in turn brought human life to Him. I considered it an honor. Now I would have two mothers, and for the rest of their lives they would receive the best I had to give.

Somehow the hours went by, and the Sabbath "rest" finally descended on Jerusalem. "How can these people rest after what they have done to the Lord of the Sabbath?" I asked myself. But there were no answers that day.

Nor would any answers come Saturday night, which seemed as endless and uncertain as Thursday night with its fear and Friday night with its shocking grief. No, we would not receive any answers until Sunday morning, when I arrived, totally out breath, at the entrance to an empty tomb.

None of us had dared believe Mary Magdalene. But Peter and I had never known her to lie to us, and she was too sensitive to pull a practical joke. Her grief had been as profound and disabling as ours.

So we went. And when we saw, we believed.

Even though His life had been restored, Jesus didn't spend much time with us after that. His physical withdrawal from us had begun, and only on a few occasions did He show Himself. But they were enough.

One morning after a discouraging night fishing on the lake, we approached the shore with no catch to show for our efforts. Those nights happen, of course, but they are never good for morale. We would have no wages that day, and on top of it, we were hungry.

Suddenly a solitary figure called out from the shore. "Have you caught anything?"

Thinking perhaps it was a merchant from town hoping to stock his market stall for the day, we regretfully shouted back, "No."

"Cast your net on the right side of the boat," came the immediate reply. "You will find some."

Incredibly, the advice proved to be correct, and we scrambled to gather in the fish that swarmed into the net, almost capsizing in the process!

"Look!" I yelled as I grabbed hold of Peter. "It's the Lord!"

He had prepared a fire and was just standing there, smiling as He waited for us to bring Him some fish. "Come and eat," He said.

Do you remember the joy you felt the first time you grasped what Jesus means to you—the first time you felt you could look into His face and "see" Him looking back at you? Well, we experienced that same joy whenever we encountered Him in person after an absence. I can't express to you how we felt as we pulled the boat up onto the beach.

And yet it would be an awkward reunion for Peter. Waiting for His moment, Jesus turned to the one who had pledged his loyalty forever, but had tossed it away under fire. "Peter, do you love Me more than these?"

It was a question that cut through flesh and muscle and fat right down to bone. Standing only a few feet away, I could feel Peter's pain.

He became defensive. "Of course, Lord! You know I love You!"

"Feed My lambs."

Silently Peter pondered this, and the rest of us pretended not to notice what was happening. Thomas elaborately stamped out the fire while Matthew made sure everyone knew he was rinsing the boat's iron skillet in the lake.

"Peter, do you love Me?"

The second query startled us. What was this? After all, Peter had answered already.

"Yes, Lord," he squirmed. "You know I love You."

"Feed My sheep."

The third time was almost too much to bear.

"Peter, do you love Me?"

My poor friend was ready to explode by now. The guilt of his betrayal, his pride, the accumulated anxiety through which all of us had come, came pouring out of him. "Lord, You know everything! And yes, You know that I love You." I thought he must be near tears.

Yes, Jesus knew. He had known all along.

"Peter, as a young man you have made your own choices and taken care of yourself. But when you are old, you will have to go where you do not wish to go."

I realize now that Jesus was making sure that Peter understood what being a first-century disciple involved. Then, when He was satisfied, He simply said, "Follow Me."

We had heard that before. The two words that would change everything. Now, after all that had happened, here was Jesus, still looking into our faces with that incomprehensible love, still saying, "Follow Me."

We were beginning to understand.

Most likely it was their mental density that kept the disciples from understanding for such a long time what their association with

Jesus was really going to cost them. It wasn't that Jesus didn't try to tell them.

"You don't know what you are asking," He had hinted darkly when the Zebedee brothers made their power play. "Can you withstand what is to come?" He probed. But they didn't get it.

He drew analogies for them, reminding them how foolish it would be to start a building project without making sure you had enough money on hand to finish it. And He pointed out the futility of going into battle unless you were sure you had the resources to win.

Finally He spoke even more directly. "You cannot be My disciple unless you are willing to leave everything else behind, including your mother and father, your wife and children, your brothers and sisters."

What did He mean by such a radical claim? On its surface it doesn't even sound like Christian behavior as we understand it, does it? I think William Barclay explains it best in his commentary on the Gospel of Luke: "We must not take his words with cold and unimaginative literalness. Eastern language is always as vivid as the human mind can make it. When Jesus tells us to hate our nearest and dearest, he does not mean that literally. He means that no love in life can compare with the love we must bear to him" (p. 196).

A lot of people who describe themselves as Christians follow Christ, all right—just at a safe distance. They're the ones at the back of the crowd. If you want to think of it that way, they're still in God's "presence," but the situation is less demanding back there. As a result, they don't really have to focus on what He is saying at any given time—indeed, they often can't hear Him. As for the cost of being a disciple . . . what's that?

Peter experienced the true cost. Saul helped impose a heavy cost on Stephen, then as Paul, eventually paid it himself. Centuries later the Waldenses carried the bloodstained banner—stained, that is, with both His blood and theirs. In modern times we have had heroes such as Dietrich Bonhoeffer, the Christian theologian executed by the Nazis. Cassie Bernall paid the price in the library at Columbine High School.

All of us pay a price, even those of us never called to lay down our lives. We pay a price by *being willing* to pay that price. "Yes, I will follow," we tell Jesus, "whatever that means and wherever it takes me."

When Jesus looked into Peter's eyes and said, "Feed My lambs," He was talking about you. But He was also speaking to you. For you are the Peter and the Matthew and the Andrew and the Mary Magdalene of the twenty-first century. If you choose to be.

chapter 17

Epilogue

They tell me I leave tomorrow. I had thought I would be on this island until my eyes closed in death. But maybe God has more work for me to do. I believe I will go over into Asia Minor, perhaps to Ephesus. Letters from the church there invite me to make my home among them in my final days.

As I looked out to sea earlier this evening, I gazed into a gigantic orange sun dipping inch by inch into the watery horizon. Suddenly, without effort on my part, I was seeing a similar sunset 70-some years ago from the eastern shore of Galilee. The others in our group weren't far away, but He was speaking almost in a whisper, directly in my ear. "John," He said, "you're so young. Your life stretches ahead of you. Are you sure this is what you want? What are you going to do for Me?"

It was true, of course. I was the youngest one He had chosen. Most of the others had become established in an occupation. I had known only my father's fishing boats and had no idea what lay ahead.

"Of course, Lord," I responded with hardly a thought. "This is exactly what I want. I want to be with You."

Now I am an old man. A life of travel and hardship has taken a huge toll. This island prison has been lonely. All the people I have loved are gone. Would I really make that choice if I were that age again?

Knowing Jesus as a personal friend and mentor in my youth was an experience few others ever had. Rising every morning just as He returned from a session with His Father, seeing His face as it still radiated from that contact with heaven, changed me in ways I never realized at the time.

I am the only one left who watched Him walk across the lake, heard Him call Jairus's little girl back to life, experienced that terrible Passover weekend in Jerusalem, saw His empty tomb two days later. And I am the last one living who saw Him rise into the clouds.

There is so much more I could tell you. I believe that if everything Jesus did for people were written down, there wouldn't be room on the earth for all the books it would take! Think of every story about Him you have ever heard, every song you have ever sung. Yet there is so much more!

Why would you want to be a young disciple of Jesus? Just as He came to me on that fishing pier, He comes to you. He needs you, too.

Why would you want to spend your life with Him? Because whatever you've heard about Him, you've only touched the surface! There is adventure waiting of which you haven't dreamed!

Why would you want to make this commitment? Because He was God who looked like you, walked on earth to be like you, understands you, gave Himself to save you.

This is my witness to you as you read these lines: I knew Him. I saw these things. I know they are true. Jesus came to me beside a fishing boat when I was not expecting Him. He may come to you in a very unlikely place at a very inconvenient time. The time and place can't be

predicted. But the invitation cannot be mistaken. He always says,
"Come, follow Me."

What will you say?

Ever wonder if those "little red books" might be useful for something other than hitting you over the head?

Video program hosts Betsy and Curtis invite you to take a brand-new look at Ellen White and her books. Join them as they travel across the country asking well-known Adventist professionals, such as José Rojas and Ben Carson, how her writings have impacted their lives. You'll meet young Adventists who have discovered the relevancy of her counsel on careers, relationships, and health, and how they were led to deeper Bible study and a closer connection with Jesus.

Video: 0-8280-1791-3
US$14.95, Can$22.45

Check out the book *A Call to Stand Apart*, a new paraphrase of selected Ellen White writings that challenges you to make an eternal difference.

Book: 0-8280-1695-X.
US$9.99, Can$14.99.

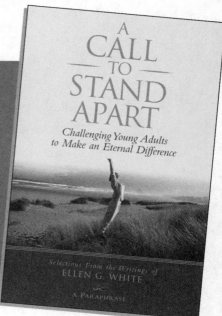